A **HOLIDAY** MAGAZINE
TRAVEL GUIDE

LONDON

The *Holiday* Guide to
LONDON

Prepared with the cooperation of the editors of HOLIDAY magazine.

RANDOM HOUSE · NEW YORK

Copyright © 1960, 1964, 1966, 1968, 1971, 1973, 1976
by The Curtis Publishing Company
All rights reserved under International and Pan-American Copyright Conventions. Published in the United States by Random House, Inc., New York, and simultaneously in Canada by Random House of Canada Limited, Toronto.

Library of Congress Cataloging in Publication Data
Main entry under title:

The Holiday guide to London.

(The Holiday magazine travel guide series ; 2)
Previous editions published under the title:
London.
Includes index.
1. London—Description—1951—Guide-books. I. Holiday. II. Series.
    DA679.L594   1976   914.21′04′857   75-40571
            ISBN 0-394-73198-0

Photographs courtesy of the British Tourist Authority

Manufactured in the United States of America
2 4 6 8 9 7 5 3
Revised Edition

CONTENTS

CHAPTER

1. HERE IS LONDON 7
  Metropolis on the Thames—her moods, her vastness, and her special delights.

2. WHAT LONDON HATH BEEN OF ANCIENT TIME 11
  The background of the city where Chaucer lived, Elizabeth ruled, the city which lived through the blitz.

3. GETTING AROUND IN LONDON 25
  Getting oriented in a city of many cities. The areas of London. The City and Westminster. Chelsea. Kensington. What is the West End?

4. LONDON DAY BY DAY 33
  Some necessary information. Aids to sightseeing. Museums and pageantry. Newspapers. Sports. Transportation. Tipping.

5. HISTORIC LONDON 57
  A guide to finding the past in London today. The Tower. Parliament. St. Paul's. Westminster and the Abbey.

6. WHERE TO STAY 77
  A selected list of hotels arranged by price and accommodations. "The Top Ten." Central London. Outskirts.

7. WHERE TO EAT IN LONDON 89
  A selection of fine restaurants—elegant or inexpensive— in each area. The Chophouses. Local and international cuisine.

8. PUBS AND WINE HOUSES 97
  A guide to places of good cheer with notes on The Local, English Beers and Opening Times.

9. ENTERTAINMENT AND NIGHT LIFE 105
  London evenings. Music, theater, ballet, or vaudeville. After the show: dancing, night clubs, and jazz or skiffle.

10. SHOPPING: FROM PINS TO ELEPHANTS 113
  What to look for and where to buy it. Shopping areas. Selected list of major stores and special shops.

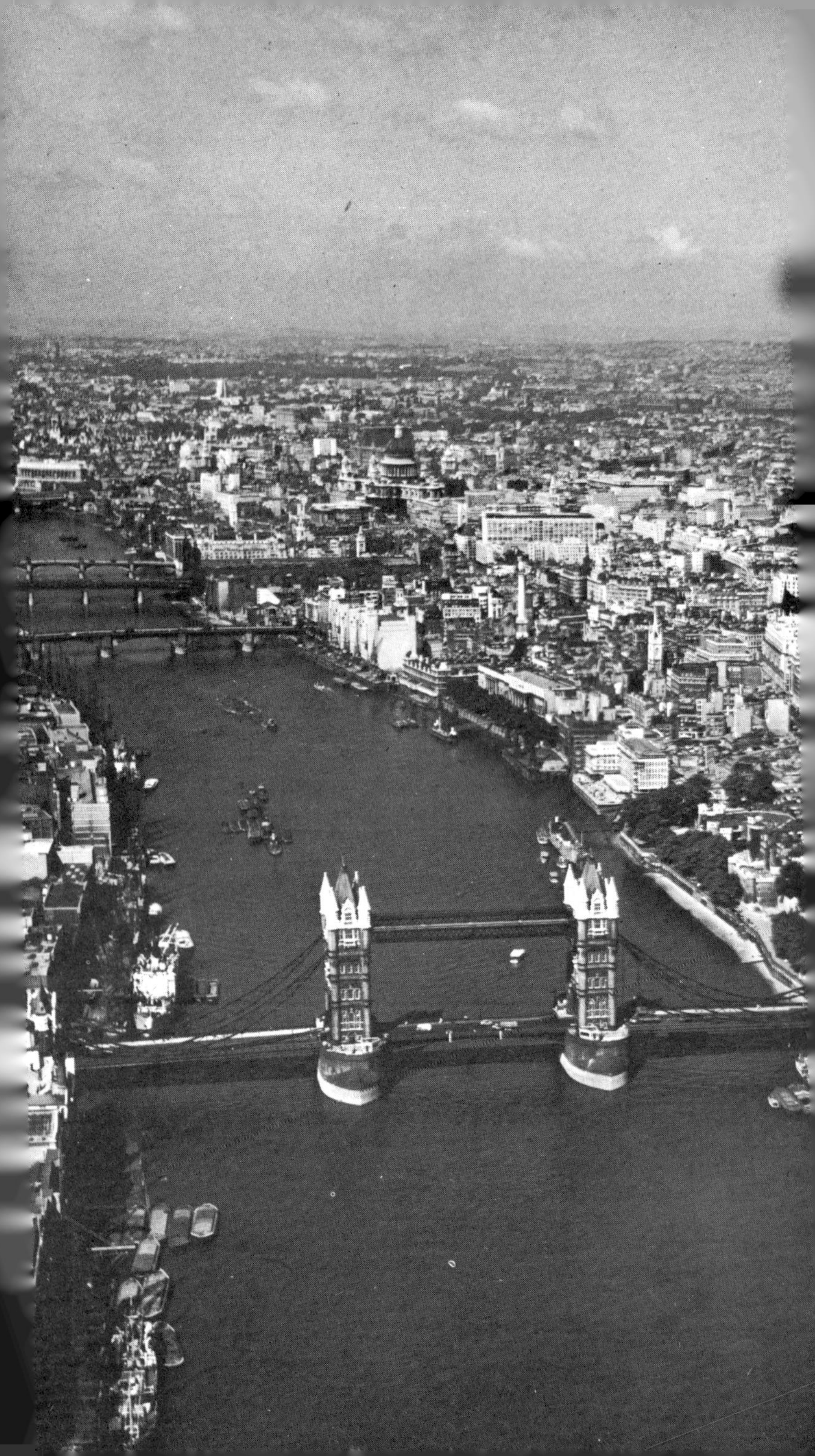

CHAPTER 1

HERE IS LONDON

Of all European cities, London holds by far the greatest number of deep-buried associations for us. Our heritage is involved in its history; we share a common past and a common culture. As children, we sang, "London Bridge Is Falling Down," and heard the tale of Dick Whittington, the poor boy with the cat, who became thrice Lord Mayor of London. Later, Mr. Pickwick, Oliver Twist, Micawber, and Little Nell brought us to the slums of London's poor, and Sherlock Holmes took us to Baker Street, shrouded in sinister fog. Shakespeare, Defoe, Shaw, Virginia Woolf—and lately, Hitchcock, Graham Greene, and Iris Murdoch—have made us citizens of a city many of us have never seen. Familiar too are Beefeaters and bobbies, Waterloo Bridge and Westminster, pubs and Piccadilly, and the Changing of the Guard at Buckingham Palace.

And so, the million and a half Americans coming to London each year are, in many ways, prepared for the great metropolis on the Thames. Yet this very familiarity can be a source of confusion. The city has figured so long in our imagination that some of our conceptions regarding it may need revising.

London has never stood still; despite its reverence for tradition it is, and always has been, in that state of perpetual ferment known as keeping up with the times. A visitor expecting to find the London of Pepys' *Diary* would obviously be in for a surprise; but so would another whose notions had been gleaned from "Upstairs, Downstairs" or "My Fair Lady." Even a returning ex-GI who had known London just after the war would find an enormous change. London as the dowdy dowager of fiction is, happily, just another myth.

For London is, above all else, a world city, a thoroughly cosmo-

London: The River Thames and Tower Bridge

politan center continuously in touch with the remotest quarters of the globe. Only New York, Paris, and Rome can be classed with it in this category. At the same time it is the acknowledged focal point of a nation—as Paris is, but as New York and Rome are not. It is, of course, the political capital of the United Kingdom, and as such the seat of the British Parliament, the ancient assembly from which so many representative bodies have derived their existence. But it is also the home of that unique institution, the British Monarchy. In this respect London is the actual, if unofficial, capital of the Commonwealth of Nations.

The British Empire may be rather close to final dissolution, but it is instructive to note that of the far-flung territories which used to be colored pink on prewar maps of the world—a quarter of the earth's land area and population—quite a few have elected to stay within this loose confederation, bound by token or real allegiance to the British Crown. This fact provides an important clue to the Londoner's special outlook, which may be compared with that of the ordinary inhabitant of Imperial Rome, who had only to remind himself, "I am a Roman citizen," to feel on top of the world. The British code of behavior being what it is, you will probably never hear a Londoner speak those sentiments out loud. He may not even entertain them consciously, but he is aware, at some level, that he is living in one of the great centers of the world—for many, *the* center. And while it is difficult to prove with figures, London is probably justified in claiming eminence as one of the world's foremost marts—a capital of trade and commerce.

A century ago, Oliver Wendell Holmes concluded, rather gloomily, that "No person can be said to know London. The most that anyone can claim is that he knows something of it." Needless to say, Holmes' London was a considerably smaller and simpler place than the immense urban complex of today. But the visitor with only a short time in which to "do" the town need not be discouraged; he can even take comfort in the knowledge that if he were to devote his entire life to the task, he could never complete it. Fortunately for the visitor, however, most of London's major points of interest lie within a fraction of the vast expanse embraced by Greater London.

Geographically, London is an immense, sprawling, not easily definable area about a nucleous called the City, which occupies a small area on the left (north) bank of the Thames. The "City" has its own Lord Mayor and is roughly analogous to New York's Wall Street district in that it is at once the oldest part of the metropolis and the headquarters of its banks and brokerage houses. Ringing the City is Greater London, administered by the Greater London Council; over the years, this area has spread out and cancelled old boundaries, having absorbed Middlesex, as well as large chunks sliced from the surrounding counties of Kent, Surrey, Essex, and Hertfordshire. The 610

In spring the gold of daffodils borders the Mall

square miles covered by this gigantic web of buildings, parks, and thoroughfares amount to more than twice the size of Greater New York. London's population, however, somewhere around 7,167,000, is less.

This contrast explains a significant feature of London: the comparative openness of its physical layout. Among the abiding joys of London are the innumerable plots given over to grass, shrubs, trees, and flowers—green oases that extend a refreshing welcome to visitors weary of walking and sight-seeing. Too small, for the most part, to be indicated on maps, these gardens, public and private, offer too the charm and enchantment of discovery. And if you were to enter a house in almost any residential quarter of the city, the chances are that behind it you would come upon a patch of lawn enclosed within neat borders of flowers and vines. The Englishman's passion for growing things is proverbial, and Londoners typically bring as much of the country as possible into town with them.

So here is London—proud but friendly, serene yet ceaselessly active, steeped in the past and yet in step with the present. It is almost overwhelming in its vastness and yet, because it is constructed and laid out on a human scale, curiously livable. As we approach the metropolis that Heinrich Heine considered "the greatest wonder which the world can show to the astonished spirit," what shall we select as our starting point? Shall it be the broad, winding river which gave it birth, and from whose wharves a band of merchant adventurers sailed to plant the first American settlement at Jamestown? Or shall it be Westminster Abbey, the national shrine, final resting place of kings and poets? Shall we begin at the Tower of London, scene of so many noble tragedies that changed the course of history; or do we prefer to start in Hyde Park beside the peaceful waters of the Serpentine? What of Piccadilly Circus? Or Nelson's column? Or Parliament? Or any of the huge Victorian railway stations?

Plainly, there can be no one answer that will satisfy everyone. The choice must depend on the mood, temperament, and preferences of the individual visitor, for surely no city is more various or more lavish with its surprises. As Dr. Johnson said: "When a man is tired of London he is tired of life; for there is in London all that life can afford."

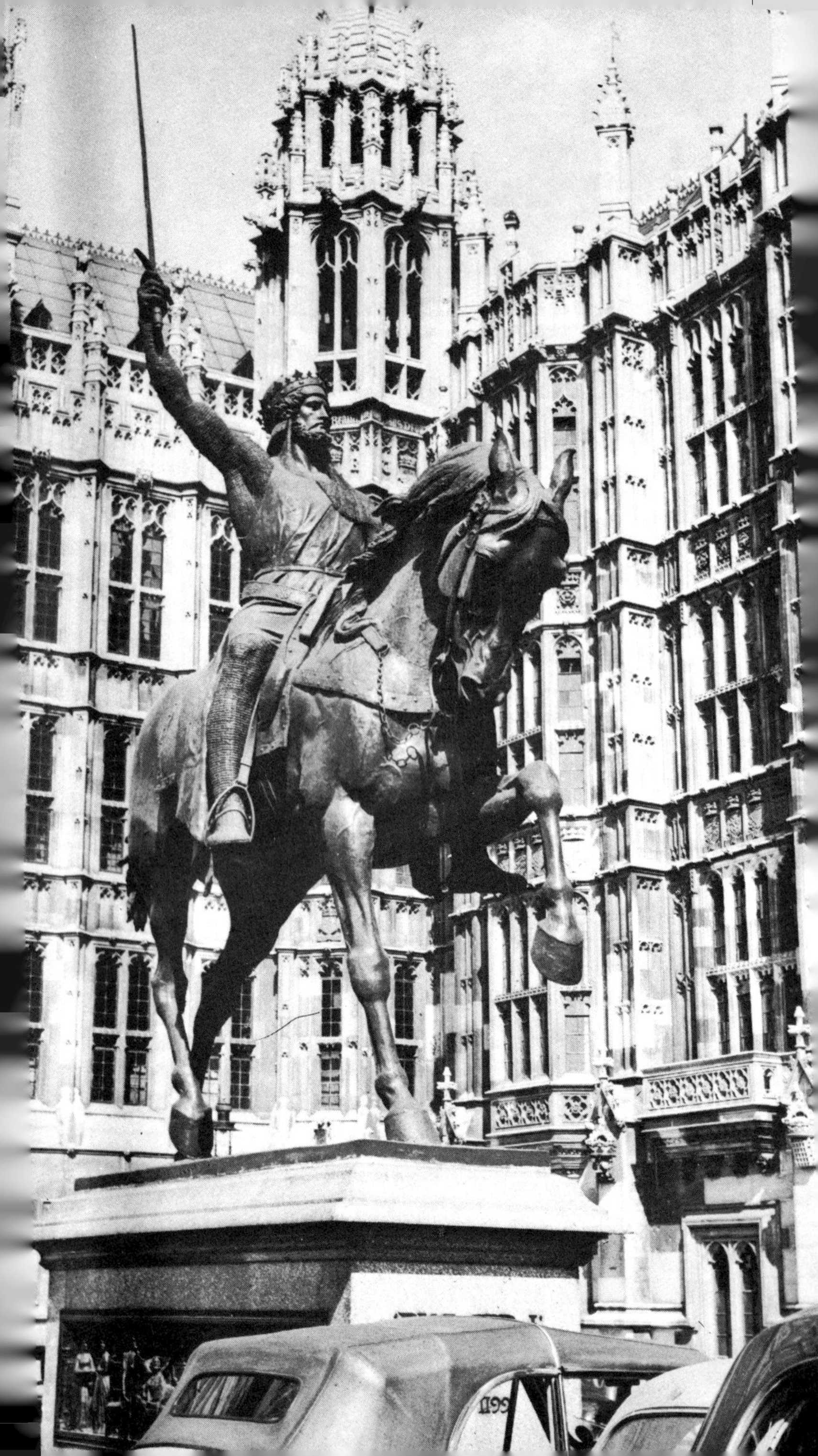

CHAPTER 2

WHAT LONDON HATH BEEN OF ANCIENT TIME

Many cities got off to earlier and more promising starts than London, but few can claim a subsequent series of events so rich in incident or crowded by so colorful a cast of characters. London's history is, of course, central to the history of England, and of the English-speaking peoples generally. It is the key to the first and the touchstone of the second. The past survives on every side in London, not only in the names and shapes of things, but in the very habits by which the city lives. Here, history provides clues to much that is otherwise baffling, for nowhere else in Britain can the national predilection for preserving traditional forms be more readily observed. This applies in particular to the pageantry—formal and informal, deliberate and unconscious—which makes up so great a part of the Londoners' daily round.

Appropriately enough for a city sometimes shrouded in fog, the actual birth of London is a mystery. Julius Caesar arrived in Britain in 55 B.C., and because that indefatigable note-taker neglected to mention London, some historians have assumed it did not exist. Others, however, point out that its site might well have recommended itself to primitive Britons as it later did to civilized Romans—and for the same reasons. For here the Thames narrowed suddenly; there were two low hills on the north bank (Ludgate Hill and Cornhill) to afford protection, and a number of useful streams flowing into the river. The name of the place, Latinized as Londinium, is certainly Celtic, though scholars dispute whether it was derived from *londo*, wild, or *lin-din,* a pool and a hill. One point on which everyone agrees, however, is that the town owed its rise to its convenience as a bridgehead for traffic to and from ports on the Continent.

Richard I, at the House of Lords

12   London

Between 43 and 50 A.D. Roman legions subjugated southeast Britain. The first recorded mention of London, by Tacitus, came in 61 A.D., when Boadicea, queen of the Iceni tribe, laid the city waste and massacred its inhabitants. The Romans struck back, crushing the revolt, whereupon Queen Boadicea committed suicide. Though her brief reign can hardly be said to have been entirely salubrious, some 70,000 Londoners having been put to the sword, the city has long since forgiven her on grounds of higher patriotism. This warrior queen is, in fact, commemorated in a spirited piece of statuary at the north end of Westminster Bridge.

The invaders continued to sway this region for another three and a half centuries, ruling the posterity of Boadicea and others with a firm but not unkindly hand. At London, the Romans raised a good-sized city, with roads radiating to other (and more important) centers. They built a wooden bridge across the river, a wide forum, a fine and spacious basilica. And, as winter-time-visitors never tire of reminding Londoners huddled over heaters and open fires, the houses of Roman London were equipped with central heating and abundant hot water.

The Romans are chiefly remembered for the protective wall—nine feet thick, twenty feet high, and three miles in circumference—with which they ringed the town. Only a few fragments remain, but many a street still follows the course it dictated. Its gates, long since dismantled, are recalled in familiar place names like Aldgate, Newgate, and Cripplegate.

In the 5th century, faraway Rome, besieged by barbarian hordes, withdrew her legions from Britain. London disappears from the record. The mist obscuring the city's fortunes is briefly pierced by the Venerable Bede, who described the town, about 730 A.D., as "the mart of many nations resorting to it by sea and land."

In the 9th and 10th centuries, England, having been overrun by Picts, Scots, Saxons, and Franks, fell prey to invasions of warlike Danes, Swedes, and Norsemen. For the most part, London managed to maintain its independence, but in 1013 the Danish raider, Sweyn,

The Boadicea Monument and Big Ben

History's stage setting: the Tower of London

captured the city. The Londoners withheld their allegiance from Sweyn's son, Canute, the unsuccessful wave-stopper of legend; but when their own candidate expired, they had no choice but to "make a truce with the army and buy themselves a peace." Their tribute of £10,500 was a full eighth of the amount paid by the entire kingdom, a fact which underlines London's wealth and predominant position.

Upstream from the city, the Thames-side place called Westminster (i.e., the monastery to the west) had for centuries slowly been growing in importance, when Edward the Confessor, king and saint, established his palace there. Later monarchs were to confirm his wisdom by following his example. While it was certainly a good idea for the ruler to live within easy reach of the country's wealthiest center, it was madness to stay within its jurisdiction: the proud and prickly Londoners had already given ample proof of their determination to defend their privileges, and were to do so again on numerous occasions for centuries to come.

In 1066 the beloved King Edward died, and was buried at Westminster in the great Abbey he had had erected there. Saxon Harold promptly seized the throne and had himself crowned in the Abbey —the first English king to do so. On hearing of this, Duke William of Normandy, Edward's cousin, angrily laid plans to recoup what he felt was his rightful inheritance. After slaying his rival at Hastings and scattering his followers, Duke William received the submission of London and had himself crowned, in turn, in "King Edward's church."

Thus, within a short space of months, two lasting traditions were established. Westminster Abbey was the burial place of practically all English monarchs until George III, and has continued to be the setting of coronations to the present day.

The Conqueror made two significant contributions to London. He granted its citizens a charter—preserved today in the Guildhall—confirming them in the enjoyment of their laws and making their city the equivalent of a shire. Then, to overawe them, he built an impregnable castle—the White Tower of the Tower of London—placing it strategically at the city's water gate.

State coaches in Royal Mews, Buckingham Palace

The Tower was enlarged by William's son, William Rufus, who also built Westminster Hall, near the Abbey. These projects cost money. Most of it came out of the coffers of London's rich merchants, who took the lesson to heart. When William Rufus died, they attached stiff conditions to their promise of support, in the election to the throne, of William's brother, Henry. The latter, as Henry I, duly granted the Londoners a new charter, which not only expanded their liberties but also bestowed on them the County of Middlesex to farm. They were even allowed to choose their own shire-reeve, or sheriff, while all others were, as a matter of course, nominated by the king. Sheriffs, incidentally, were like dictatorial state governors: they levied taxes, collected fines, and saw to the military organization of their counties.

In 1135, when Henry I died, the Londoners once again asserted their right to select the monarch, and when their candidate, Stephen, was held prisoner by partisans of Queen Matilda, they demanded his release. Their rebellion finally drove the Queen from England. It was not until much later in the same century, however, that London took its first truly important step forward on the path to liberty. Tiring of the arrogance of William Longchamp, regent for Richard I while that monarch was away at the Crusades, the Londoners struck a bargain with the king's brother, John. In 1191, the barons of England and citizens of London met at St. Paul's Cathedral and named John regent in place of Longchamp. In redemption of John's pledge, London became the first municipal corporation in England, on the model of such semi-autonomous Continental cities as Rouen, with its own mayor, elected as he is to this day from among the aldermen. The city thus acquired democratic institutions well in advance of the country at large, and its leaders were to play important roles in the struggle for representative government on a nationwide basis.

Their first opportunity came in 1215, when the barons rebelled against the tyranny of John, who had since become king. London opened its gates to their army, and its mayor, though a commoner, was made a member of the Committee of Barons appointed to see to it that the terms of Magna Carta, sealed by John at Runnymede, were faithfully carried out. That famous document, by the way, specifically directed: "Let the city of London have all its old liberties and its free customs, as well by land as by water."

John's successor, Henry III (1216–1272), envious of London's preeminence, did everything in his power to humble its pride—taxing its treasury, imposing huge fines for the most trivial offenses, and deposing its mayor no fewer than nine times. Under the circumstances it is hardly surprising that the exasperated citizens should have thrown their weight behind Simon de Montfort, who, in 1264, finally achieved the creation of a national Parliament. While that body's powers were to be curtailed, subverted, and suspended on numerous occasions, its very creation established the principle of the people's right to an assembly through which to seek redress against the acts of an arbitrary sovereign. Remote though it is in time, this 13th-century assembly is the direct ancestor of our own Senate and House of Representatives.

In the government of London itself, the guilds—trade-wide protective organizations combining features of management cartels and labor unions—wielded increasing power as the fortunes of the city's mercantile classes steadily improved. Today, the mighty guilds are perpetuated in the City Livery Companies—the Goldsmiths, Fishmongers, Brewers, and so on.

As trade flourished and medieval London grew, the need for a dependable bridge across the Thames became more pressing. Since Roman days a succession of wooden structures had been built, only to be swept away by floods or broken down by invaders or destroyed by fire. Then, in the 12th century, a priest named Peter of Colechurch conceived the revolutionary idea of building a bridge in stone, and in 1176 he made a start. For a long time he was hampered by lack of funds, until Henry II settled on him the proceeds of a tax on wool—a circumstance which gave rise to the curious notion, believed by the credulous for centuries, that London Bridge was built on wool sacks. Actually, it was erected on stone foundations resting on wooden piles driven deep into the river's oozy bed.

The work was fraught with danger, for as each new pier was set in place the current raced still more swiftly through the narrow arches: altogether 200 workmen were drowned. Peter himself died in 1205, and was laid to rest in a church on the central pier dedicated to Thomas à Becket, called Thomas of London. Nearly a third of a century after building had begun, the bridge was complete. It was 906 feet long and 20 feet wide, with a drawbridge to allow ships to pass: an engineering marvel without precedent since the great architectural triumphs of the Romans.

16 London

Soon, houses and shops began to spring up along the new structure, their backs jutting precariously out over the water. The bridge became a haunt of high fashion. Apparently it remained so, for three centuries after it was opened, Norden describes it as being adorned "with sumptuous buildings and stately and beautiful houses on either side, inhabited by wealthy citizens, and furnished with all manner of trades, comparable in itself to a little city." If we remember that the bridge was bustling London's only link with the south, we should be less surprised to learn that people passing over it at peak hours were quite likely to be crushed to death, or jostled from the parapets to plummet into the turbulent waters below.

What *is* surprising is that it was not until 1750 that a second span (the first Westminster Bridge) was built to help relieve the congestion. And not until 1832 was Peter's old structure at last pulled down, after six centuries of use.

In the 14th and 15th centuries, although serfdom was in revolt and Kentish rebels such as Wat Tyler (1381) and Jack Cade (1450) marched on the capital, business continued to flourish. When Henry VIII—shrewd, greedy, ruthless, and fiercely nationalistic—came to the throne in 1509, he was a king after the hearts of London's businessmen. He dealt a body blow to feudal restraints and opened the way to commercial expansion free of ecclesiastical restrictions. The enormous treasure which Henry seized from the Church after his rupture with Rome enabled him, moreover, to ease the financial pressure on London's moneyed classes—a move which certainly did him no harm in their eyes.

Relics of medieval warfare in the Tower Armory

The stocks, a once popular device for the correction of criminals

Henry's daughter Mary, however, reversed this trend. Her zealous attempts to restore the old religion earned her the abiding hatred of the populace and the sobriquet "Bloody," which has clung to her name ever since.

The long reign of Elizabeth I (1558–1603) was accompanied by tremendous growth—of London itself no less than of the country's fortunes at home and abroad. In 1580, the Queen, desirous of more space for the city, prohibited all new building within three miles of the walls. This edict stimulated the construction, by wealthy merchants, nobles, and churchmen, of spacious and splendid country houses, particularly to the west along the river. Here can be seen the beginnings of commuting, with the Thames serving as the natural highway linking home with place of business. Even for short trips within the City, the river was used in preference to the narrow, unpaved streets, which were frequently littered with garbage and cluttered with cattle, carts, and petty criminals.

Like as not, a traveler's destination would be one of the new theatres—perhaps the Globe, on the south bank, where crude spectacles like bear-baiting competed for favor with the latest dramatic works of a talented actor-manager named William Shakespeare. Since 1576, when James Burbage had built the country's first playhouse in Shoreditch, just north of London, the stage had become extremely popular; with brief interruptions it has continued to play a vital role in the life of London to this day.

In 1603, Queen Elizabeth died, and King James VI of Scotland ascended the throne as James I. A large migration of his countrymen came to London in his wake. Under his son, Charles I, the great architect Inigo Jones introduced town planning—in a city whose population had tripled in the past century and by 1640 stood at about 400,000. This development was soon halted, however, by civil war. Charles, who had antagonized the City's leaders with a series of dubious devices for replenishing the royal exchequer, had few friends left in London when war threatened. When a large body of Londoners at Turnham Green helped Lord Essex to force the King to retire, London never saw him again until he was tried at Westminster and executed there in January, 1649.

18 London

It was at Westminster, too, that Oliver Cromwell had himself proclaimed Lord Protector of England—not in the Abbey but in Westminster Hall, whither the Coronation Chair was brought for the purpose. Once in command, the Puritans lost no time in destroying "idolatrous" relics of the past, including most notably the Eleanor's Cross, which had stood for centuries at the village of Charing, between Westminster and the City, and from which Charing Cross took its name. On moral grounds they banned plays and other public entertainments—"the devil's work," they called them—and the life of London became infinitely more austere than it had been.

Even so, joy was by no means universal when, in 1660, the Stuart dynasty was restored to power in the person of Charles II. A few years later, however, the city was visited by twin calamities of such overwhelming horror as to efface the partisan struggle for the time being. These disasters were the Great Plague of 1665–66 and the Great Fire of 1666.

In common with other European centers London had known the Black Death on a number of occasions during the Middle Ages. There had been serious outbreaks too in 1603 and 1625, but it is probable that London's last visitation was also its worst. Over 90,000 men, women, and children perished in agony. Uncounted others, fleeing the city, died of exposure and starvation.

Finally, the pestilence waned. It would certainly have returned to London with renewed virulence if it had not been for the Great Fire. This terrible conflagration was probably the greatest blessing ever to fall upon London, for it cleansed that immense pesthouse with total efficiency. In four fantastic days, the flames consumed the infected habitations of rich and poor, scourged the filth of centuries, purified the germ-infested soil, and buried beneath tons of smoking debris the disease-laden streams and open sewers. Thirteen thousand houses disappeared; a fifth of a million people were made homeless; five-sixths of the city lay in ruins. But the plague had been stopped.

The Rebuilding Act of 1667 directed that, instead of wood, brick and stone only should be used, and the London that gradually emerged from the ashes was a far more orderly place, in appearance at any rate, than its picturesque predecessor.

It was not, to be sure, as nobly laid out as it would have been had Christopher Wren's master plan been adopted. The great astronomer-architect envisaged a grand city of broad, straight avenues. Conservatism carried the day, however, and for the most part London's new streets faithfully followed the old courses. Wren's mighty talents were nevertheless employed for decades in designing an astonishing number of churches, public buildings, and private homes in and around the metropolis, most of which can still be seen. To many people Wren's finest triumph was St. Paul's Cathedral.

Wren's patron, Charles II (1660–1685), is remembered as the Merry Monarch for his amorous escapades; and the morals of Lon-

Ravens are the Tower's oldest and most welcome tenants

don's fashionable world, as mirrored in the Restoration comedies of Congreve, Wycherley, and others, sank to new depths during his reign. Playboys and courtesans abounded in the elegant quarter then springing up beyond the City's western walls, and still known as the West End. Yet the well-to-do "solid citizens" were far from abandoning the pursuit of profit for that of pleasure. Samuel Pepys, the diarist, exemplifies this: a canny, hardheaded cloth merchant, he was also a gay courtier and *bon vivant,* and while he gamed, tippled, and wenched with the best (and worst) of London society, he rarely failed to note to the penny exactly how much each of his carefree capers had cost him.

When King Charles died, with the name of his favorite mistress, Nell Gwyn, on his lips, he was succeeded by his unloved brother, the Duke of York. As James II, that worthy added one small but significant feature to the local skyline: a weather vane which he caused to be placed atop the Banqueting House in Whitehall, so that he might know which way the wind was blowing while he nervously awaited the approach of William, Prince of Orange, from the Netherlands.

The moment was not long in coming. In 1688, at the invitation of the country's leading citizens, Prince William arrived, and James fled to exile in France. Both events produced considerable satisfaction in London. The following year, King William III purchased Kensington Palace, in what was then a charmingly rustic spot westward from the metropolis; there, twelve years later, he died, as did his successor, Queen Anne, another twelve years after that. The first two Georges stayed at Kensington from time to time, but George III deserted it in favor of other royal residences.

Not one of these stodgy and predominantly Teutonic sovereigns was noted for style, or even suspected of imagination. Yet the society of their time was one of exceptional brilliance. London, more than ever the center of things, drew to itself a swarm of writers, artists, politicians, poets, and men of talent from every corner of the kingdom. The metropolis tingled with the wit of Dryden, Pope, Swift, and the inimitable Dr. Johnson. Fox, Burke, and the two Pitts scored triumphs in Parliament, and set a new standard of genius in government. The stage thrived as it had not since Elizabethan times. In an age of innovations, London witnessed the emergence of the first

20 London

Prime Minister (Robert Walpole), the first novel (Richardson's *Pamela*), and, with Reynolds, Gainsborough, and Hogarth, the first distinctly English school of painting.

Early in the 18th century coffee houses appeared in London, becoming at once the haunt of literary lions and cubs, playwrights, statesmen, and men with ideas in search of a sympathetic audience. The noblemen and rich gentry preferred their clubs. Brain-stimulating coffee was the drink of the first group and gout-producing port that of the second; but the tipple of the common people was gin, available in quantity at very low prices. The havoc wrought by it in the junglelike slums of London is memorably portrayed in the famous drawing "Gin Lane," sketched with savage humor by Hogarth.

Below the calm and ordered surface London in the Augustan Age was a vast cesspool pullulating with vice and crime. Law-abiding citizens scarcely dared venture into the unlighted streets after dark. Where were the police? There were none—only a loosely organized body known as the watch.

The law, meanwhile, compounded lawlessness by decreeing the penalty of death by hanging for a whole catalogue of offenses, two hundred in all. This naturally encouraged criminals to perpetrate the most violent acts, which promised the biggest immediate rewards.

But lawlessness was not confined to the lower orders; it infected all classes. The series of stock frauds in 1720 which resulted in the

Where sense and wit held sway: Dr. Johnson's house

calamitous wave of speculation known as the South Sea Bubble was only the most spectacular of many financial scandals. Among rich aristocrats gambling was endemic: the disease often proved fatal, for by the code of honor that obtained, a gentleman who was unable to pay his debts could only atone by taking his life. In the Army, the Navy, and the Church, high offices were bought and sold.

As to the theatre, then becoming established in and around Covent Garden, it too had its share of scandals. Though it boasted such illustrious names as Garrick, Sheridan, and Mrs. Siddons, the play-goer was by no means sure of getting his money's worth. The most famous theatrical swindle occurred in 1749. On the evening of January 16 a huge crowd assembled in the Haymarket Theatre in response to an announcement stating that a performer would insert himself in a quart bottle and sing a repertoire of popular songs, allowing people in the audience to handle the bottle containing him as he did so. Expectation was intense. Time passed, and as the performer failed to appear, the crowd became restive. At last a voice shouted from behind the curtain that if the spectators would kindly stay in their seats until the following evening he would get into a *pint* bottle for their entertainment. Howling with rage, the mob rioted, and within minutes completely demolished the inside of the theatre.

During the 18th century, London finally lost its character as a walled city. The remaining sections of the Roman wall were pulled down and the medieval gates dismantled and sold. To the fury of the watermen, hackney cabs multiplied, and the Thames ceased to be the city's main thoroughfare. Streets became wider and longer, and were paved with cobblestones. The malodorous Fleet River, of which Pope had written as rolling "its tribute of dead dogs to Thames," was covered over to make Fleet Street. Many important buildings went up, including Mansion House (the Lord Mayor's residence) and the Horse Guards. Soane, Chambers, and the Adam brothers made magnificent countributions to the city's architecture, and Bloomsbury was laid out in garden squares, setting a model for future developers from which generations of Londoners were to benefit.

Meanwhile, the city grew rapidly outward, so that by 1801, when the first decennial census showed a population of 864,845, it covered forty square miles. The historic mile-square central area still numbered 156,859 souls (as opposed to 5,000 today) and was separated from much of the rest by green fields and dusty tracks. The advent of the Industrial Revolution greatly hastened London's expansion: by 1873 the city had tripled in size and quadrupled in population, to 115 square miles and 3,300,000 people. It was customary, by this time, to refer to old London as the City, with a capital *C*.

The 19th century, an age of reform, brought sweeping changes in swift succession. In 1828, Sir Robert Peel, the Home Secretary, introduced a multitude of long-overdue improvements in the administration of justice; the best-remembered of these was the creation of a

London, The Royal Naval College

metropolitan police force, whose top-hatted members were promptly dubbed "bobbies" in honor of their founder. In 1836, the first railway train departed from a London terminus; it chugged from London Bridge to Greenwich, a distance of six miles. The following year, at five o'clock in the morning of June 20, two gentlemen called at Kensington Palace to inform eighteen-year-old Princess Victoria that she had become Queen of England; a few weeks later she took up residence in Buckingham Palace, the first English monarch to do so. In 1851, she and her beloved consort, Prince Albert, opened the Great Exhibition in Hyde Park, which set the style for subsequent international exhibitions elsewhere. Nine years later, London's first tramway opened, connecting Marble Arch and Bayswater.

Gradually, the London of Dickens gave way to the London of Conan Doyle—and of Whistler, the Rossettis, Wildes, and the "Yellow Book" group. In 1871, came the Albert Hall; in 1891, a telephone link with Paris; and in 1894, that curiously fascinating structure, Tower Bridge. G. B. Shaw was the town's most prolific playwright. In 1901, London mourned the death of Queen Victoria and cheered the accession of her son Edward VII. The period called Edwardian came into flower, only to end, technically at any rate, with the King's death in 1910. George V ascended the throne. In 1913, there were many disorders arising from the efforts of suffragist women to attract attention to their cause. In 1914, the country went to war.

During the First World War, London was attacked from overseas for the first time since 1066. Raids by German Zeppelins and aircraft killed 524 people, injured 1,264, and caused damage estimated at about £2,000,000. Shortly after the Armistice, Viscount Trenchard, speaking in the House of Lords, predicted that the number of bombs dropped on Britain during the course of the entire conflict would, in the next war, "be dropped in six hours, continuously for five or six weeks." Terrifying as this prophecy must have seemed at the time, it turned out, on fulfillment, to have been somewhat short of the mark.

For the war which followed the General Strike of 1926 and the Abdication Crisis ten years later, lasted not six weeks but six years; and London, instead of being a remote target, was steadily and relentlessly bombarded, month after punishing month, from enemy bases within easy range. The capital sustained its greatest loss of life since the Plague, and its greatest damage to property since the Fire of 1666. In this, Britain's "finest hour," the Londoners showed their mettle. Acts of heroism became so common that only the most extraordinary were commented on.

Between June and October 1944 came the second phase, when the "doodlebugs" rained on the metropolis. This campaign was trying to morale but nothing in comparison to the third phase, from October 1944 until March 1945, a month before the German surrender. While they were less nerve-racking than the "doodlebugs" or V.1 rocket bombs, the V.2s were infinitely more deadly. At least 1,050 of these huge missiles were aimed at London, and though many fell short or exploded in mid-air, a high percentage found their mark. Altogether, these "revenge" weapons, whose use could hardly have affected the outcome of the war, took the lives of 8,436 Londoners.

London's total civilian roll of honor from air raids throughout the war amounted to 29,890 dead and 50,497 seriously hurt. No fewer than 242,764 houses in Greater London had been destroyed or seriously damaged, and 700,000 required repairs. To reckon the loss in terms of pounds, shillings and pence was quite impossible, since so much that was beyond price was gone forever.

Slowly, London set about the task of rebuilding. In 1952, the city mourned the death of its wartime king and comrade, George VI. With the accession of his daughter Elizabeth London continued to heal its physical and economic wounds. By the 1960's, the tempo of London's life had quickened.

And in the 1970's, London has become a "swinging" city—*the* center of pop culture and instant fashion, as well as theater, opera, and other mainstays of "civilization." New architecture sprouts among the old, often in the form of hotels to house the overwhelming influx of tourists. A decisive step for England was her entrance into the Common Market which binds her more closely than ever to the rest of Europe, and London is now perhaps more cosmopolitan than ever. But despite modern sophistication on one hand, and quintessential British tradition on the other, the unique atmosphere of London has recently begun to reflect the country's troubled economic position and the ominous political problem of Northern Ireland.

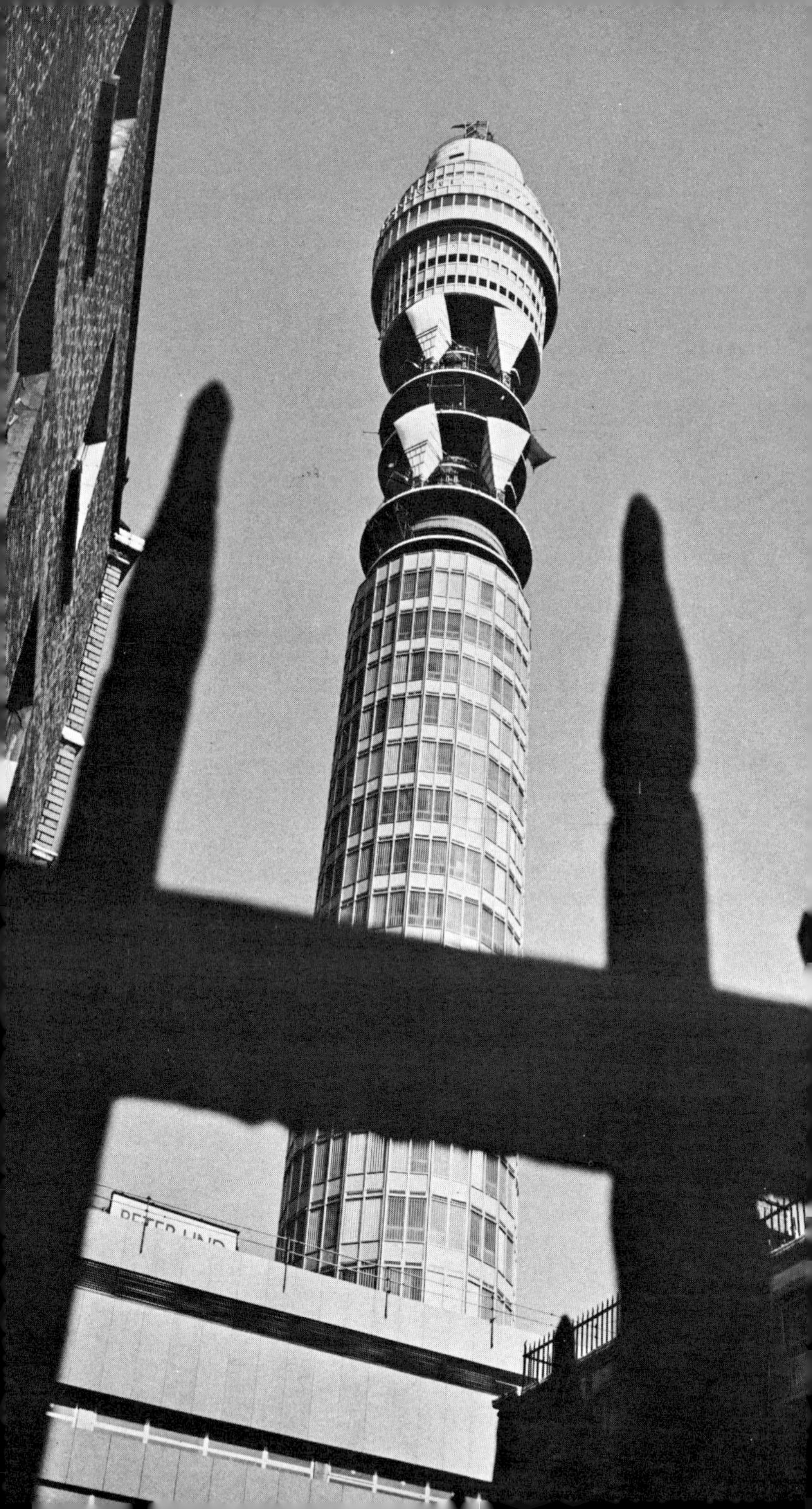

CHAPTER *3*

GETTING AROUND IN LONDON

Los Angeles may or may not be the biggest village in the world, but London can certainly lay claim to being the biggest *collection* of villages. American cities have their "uptowns" and "downtowns"; many have numbered streets; and in most, orientation is made easy by the use of points of the compass to describe a district's location with respect to the center (e.g., Chicago's "South Side" or Washington's familiar "N.W."). In conglomerate London, unfortunately, none of these aids is present. The designating letters of the postal districts convey, it is true, the general direction of a given point from General Post Office headquarters in the City, but the number tells nothing of its distance therefrom. Perhaps the only landmark which, because of its height, would give the visitor a reassuring sense of just where he is, is the Post Office Tower, altogether 620 feet high and visible from most everywhere. The panoramic view from the top of the tower, which you can see by having lunch there, should help you get a general bearing on the confusing metropolis below.

GETTING ORIENTED

The map just at the end of this book covers the most central sections of London. By referring to it along with this chapter you will be able to orient yourself in terms of the places you are going to see, and the place names you are going to be dealing with.

But because of London's size, you might want to purchase a larger map, and many are available at magazine stands and branches of W. H. Smith. The Map Productions one is excellent; the Automobile Association publishes a reversible Inner and Outer London map,

The new Post Office Tower rises above the old London

The City (E.C.2, E.C.3, E.C.4). This is not only the ancient heart of London but also, in terms of finance and trade, the heart of Britain and the entire Commonwealth. This celebrated "square mile" stretches along the north bank of the Thames, with the Conqueror's Tower standing guard at its eastern or seaward limit. Divided into 26 wards, it is governed by a Lord Mayor and a Court of Aldermen, while the mere boroughs have only mayors and borough councils. The City has its own police force, wearing uniforms recognizably different from those of metropolitan police, and its own courts of law. Here are the Royal Exchange, the Guildhall, the Bank of England, Lloyds of London, the Old Bailey, and St. Paul's Cathedral. By day, over half a million people throng its narrow old streets, but by night it shrinks to a small town, with a residential population of only 5,000.

Southwark and Lambeth. South of the City, across the river and linked to it by London, Southwark, and Blackfriars Bridges, is the borough of Southwark (pronounced "Suth-(u)ck" with the "th" soft, as in "thou") and in particular its waterfront district of *Bankside* (S.E. 1) which contains, among its warehouses, the site of the Globe Theatre. Southwark is as old as London itself. At the southern end of

The Royal Exchange

Lambeth Palace, London home of the Archbishops of Canterbury

London Bridge stands Southwark Cathedral, where John Harvard was baptized. Farther south is the famed *Elephant and Castle* district (S.E. 1) which took its name from the Spanish Princess Infanta de Castilla.

On the west of Southwark, but, owing to a sharp bend in the river, on the *east* bank of the Thames, lies the borough of Lambeth. It is linked to Westminster by no fewer than five railway, foot-, and vehicular bridges, whose names, reading upstream or north to south, are Waterloo, Hungerford, Westminster, Lambeth, and Vauxhall. Lambeth includes Waterloo Station, the Old Vic Theatre, and London's superb architecturally intriguing arts complex—the Royal Festival Hall, Queen Elizabeth Hall, the Purcell Room, the Hayward Gallery, the National Film Theatre, and the newly built National Theatre (S.E. 1). Notable too is Lambeth Palace, the London residence of the Archbishops of Canterbury for 700 years. The Imperial War Museum and Lambeth Walk are nearby (S.E. 11).

Westminster. Four times the size of the City of London, the City (borough) of Westminster, across the river from Lambeth, occupies the greater part of the center of the metropolis. It extends three miles along the Thames, from the Temple to Chelsea Bridge; on the west it is bounded by Chelsea and Kensington, and on the north it is separated from the borough of St. Marylebone by the great east-west artery, Oxford Street. For a short distance it shares a boundary with the borough of Holborn before it again meets the City, on the east.

In practice, the term *Westminster* refers to a particular part of the whole: that quarter, extending inland from the river, which includes Wellington Barracks, the Roman Catholic Westminster Cathedral, and the Tate Gallery; but more especially Westminster Abbey, the Houses of Parliament, New Scotland Yard, and the government buildings of Whitehall. "Whitehall" connotes the Foreign Office, and "Westminster" has exactly the same signification for Britishers that "Washington, D.C." has for us: the seat of national government.

South of Piccadilly Circus, and bordered by Green Park and St. James's Park on the southwest and southeast, is the quiet and ultra-elegant quarter of *St. James's* (S.W.1) so called after the park and St. James's Palace. With its clubs and world-famous men's shops, this district is a citadel of male pride and prerogative.

Northward from Piccadilly Circus extends the fan-shaped "foreign-speaking island" of *Soho,* with its legendary restaurants.

West of Soho, from Regent Street all the way to Park Lane along Hyde Park, is fashionable *Mayfair* (W.1). The equally stylish and more exclusively residential quarter of *Belgravia* (S.W.1) lies southward and slightly to the west, on the other side of the parks, grouped around Belgrave and Eaton Squares. The mixed shopping and residential area just south of Hyde Park, where Belgravia meets Chelsea and Kensington, is called *Knightsbridge* (S.W.1 and S.W.7) after its principal thoroughfare.

Pimlico (S.W.1) is the designation still given to the territory reach-

Soho, center of London's international restaurants

Quiet streets like Cheyne Walk contrast with the City's bustle

ing northward from the river between Chelsea Bridge Road (and Chelsea) and Vauxhall Bridge Road (and Westminster). More and more frequently, however, one hears the area spoken of as *Victoria*, after its vast railway station.

Chelsea. From Chelsea Bridge, next to the Pimlico-Victoria district of the City of Westminster, the borough of Chelsea (mostly in S.W.3) reaches westward along the Thames, opposite the borough of Battersea (S.W.11) to the south, to which it is connected by the Chelsea, Albert, and Battersea Bridges, to Chelsea Creek, where it gives way to Fulham (S.W.6). The borough is separated from Kensington, to the north, by the Fulham Road, from which the boundary continues north to take in a chunk of Knightsbridge and turns south to slice from the flank of Belgravia a sliver which includes *Sloane Square* (S.W.1). From here, the King's Road runs southwest to Fulham, bisecting the borough throughout its length.

Chelsea, the chosen home and haunt of Carlyle, George Eliot, the Rossettis, and innumerable other writers, painters and actors, is one of the most charming areas of all London. Its riverfront, especially that section known as Cheyne ("Chay-nee") Walk, is of great beauty. The brilliant uniforms of the "Chelsea Pensioners"—old and disabled soldiers domiciled at Chelsea Hospital—add splashes of warm color to its streets.

Kensington. The large Royal Borough of Kensington extends northward and westward from Chelsea, with Fulham and Hammersmith on its western flank, to where it meets Paddington, north of Hyde Park. Kensington used to be almost entirely residential, but has lately been besieged with clothing boutiques and antique markets, especially along the High Street and Kensington Church Street. *South Kensington* and *Brompton* (both S.W. 7) south of Hyde Park, are only a little less prosperous than neighboring Knightsbridge and Belgravia. In this area are many museums (such as the Victoria and Albert, and the Museum of Natural History) as well as the Royal Albert Hall and the Brompton Oratory.

Earl's Court (S.W. 5) in the southeastern section is, despite its name, both solid middle class and the temporary residence of visit-

The Thames, the world's gateway to London

ing tourists from the Commonwealth; it abounds in rooming houses.

The large area between Kensington High Street and Holland Park Avenue (W. 8, *Campden Hill*) contains many fine homes and beautiful gardens, in addition to Holland Park itself. The *Notting Hill* gate (W. 11) is a lively mixture of rich and poor, young and old, and the site of the famous *Portobello* street market; it can best be described as "up and coming."

Perhaps the most important single building in the borough is Kensington Palace, the home of William of Orange and several later kings and princes, and site of the London Museum, State Apart-

Getting Around in London 31

ments and Orangery. The pleasant gardens which were once its grounds are a favorite public attraction.

Paddington and St. Marylebone. East of northern Kensington, the borough of Paddington (W.2, W.9, W.10, W.11, N.W.6) extends eastward to Marble Arch and Speakers' Corner where soapbox orators hold forth on Sunday afternoons and summer evenings. Once-fashionable *Bayswater* has had many of its famous homes turned into tourist hotels. *Queensway* abounds with restaurants and all-night supermarkets, convenient for visitors staying in the Lancaster Gate area, north of the Bayswater Road. This section has many quiet squares and noisy pubs, but nearby *Paddington* is primarily devoted to Paddington railway station.

The borough of St. Marylebone ("*Mar*-(li)b'n"), commonly called Marylebone, extends eastward from the Edgware Road and the *Marble Arch* district (W.1); on the south it faces Mayfair across Oxford Street. Among the borough's many fine streets are Sherlock Holmes's Baker Street and Harley Street, where some of the world's most distinguished physicians and surgeons maintain offices. Marylebone includes Marylebone Station, Madame Tussaud's Waxworks, the Wallace Collection (of fine art), and, in the northern district of *St. John's Wood* (N.W.8), the international home and shrine of an English sport played around the globe: Lord's Cricket Ground. East of this is *Regent's Park* (N.W.1) with its justly celebrated Zoo.

St. Pancras and Holborn. Directly east of St. Marylebone are Holborn and the Metropolitan Borough of St. Pancras. The latter has no less than three large railway termini: Euston, St. Pancras, and King's Cross. South of these is the Georgian district of *Bloomsbury* (W.C.1) with London University and the British Museum.

The commercial district of *Holborn* ("*Hoe-b'n*"—W.C.1 and E.C.1) between St. Pancras and the City, is chiefly notable for including two of the four remaining Inns of Court: Gray's Inn, with its Gardens, and Lincoln's Inn, with its Fields. Both Dickens and Dr. Johnson lived and wrote in Holborn.

What is the West End? The term "West End," which crops up so constantly in newspaper stories, advertisements, and small talk, with overtones of smartness and luxury, signifies the sizable region west of the City which takes in most of London's first-rate shops and theatres. It includes Mayfair, Soho, and St. James's, and all of the City of Westminster to the east of Trafalgar Square—the first three districts primarily for shops, the last primarily for theatres, and all for an amazing variety of restaurants, especially those in London's miniature "Chinatown."

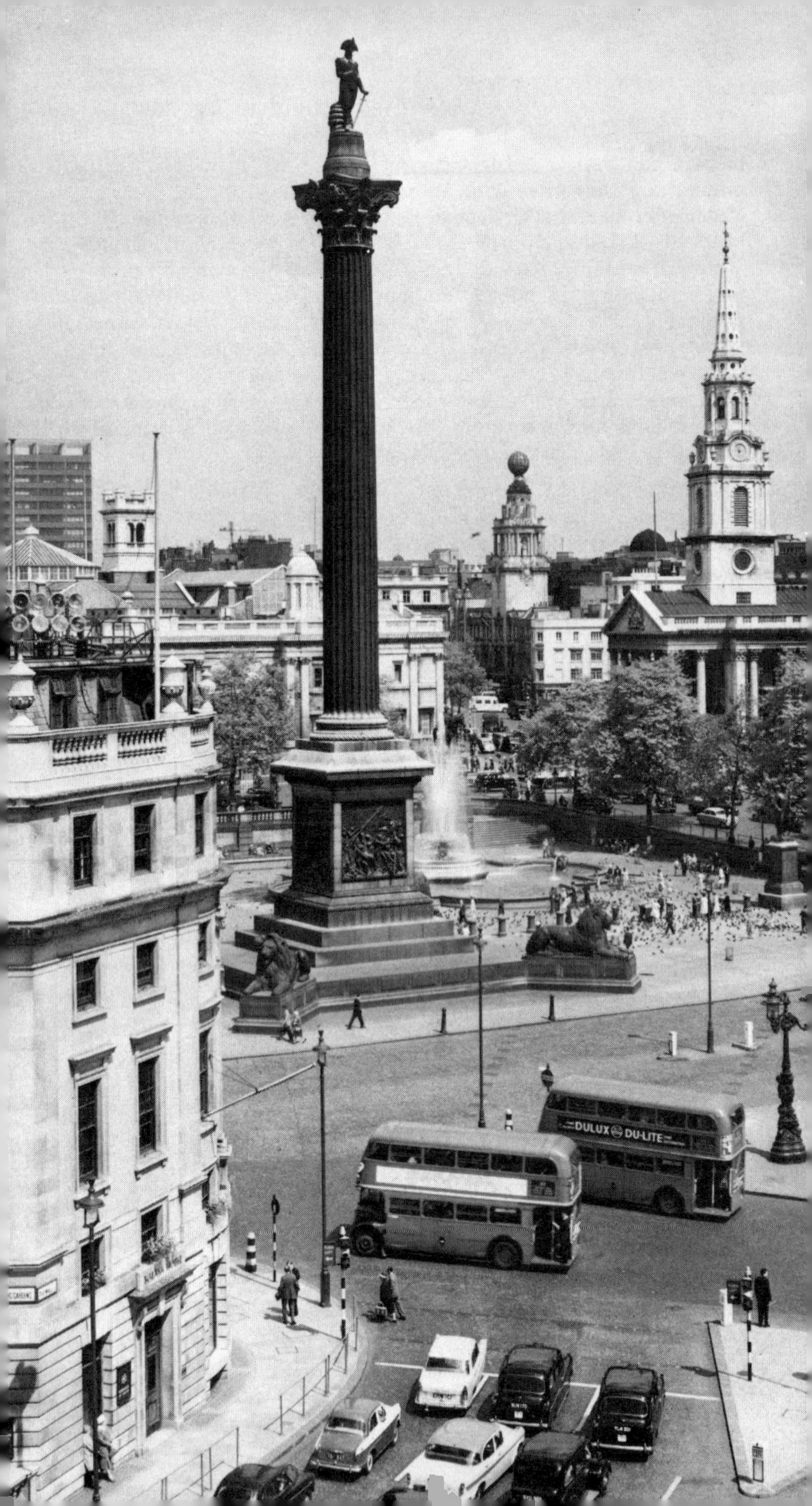
DULUX DU-LITE

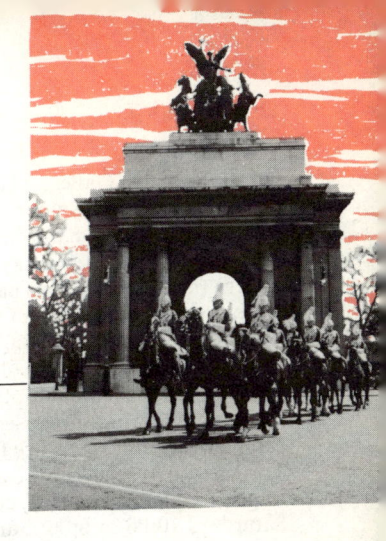

CHAPTER 4

LONDON DAY BY DAY

Like most stereotypes, the one so often drawn of London as the fog-bound home of Victorianism couldn't be further from the truth. London is one of the two or three most exciting cities of the world. This chapter lists the sights and spectacles you won't want to miss. You will also find practical hints (money, tours, transportation), useful addresses and phone numbers, and insights into Londoners's ways.

Aids to Sightseeing. The London Tourist Board (4 Grosvenor Gardens, S.W. 1, near Victoria) has brochures and answers; branch offices: Victoria Station (near platform 15) and the BOAC Air Terminal, Buckingham Palace Road. Other great sources: the British Tourist Authority (64 St. James's Street, S.W. 1; 629–9191); and American Express (6 Haymarket, S.W. 1; 930-4141). Dial 123 for the time; 246-8091 for the weather; and 246-8041 for a 2½-minute recorded report of the day's events.

Publications that might come in handy are *How to Get There* (8 p.) published by the London Transport Authority, *Visitor's London* (50 p.), and the excellent *Nicholson's London Guide* (50 p.) which includes area maps, bus and subway (called Underground in London) routes, and more specialized information. *This Month in London* (20 p.) is useful for up-to-date schedules of events, shows, sports, etc.

Art. While the British would be the last to claim a national talent for art, they have numbered among them some of the world's most enthusiastic *collectors,* ever since Henry VIII hired Hans Holbein as court painter. London's galleries are consequently crammed with art treasures of the first magnitude. Following are the most outstanding.

Nelson's Column in Trafalgar Square

The National Gallery (Trafalgar Square, W.C. 2) is one of the world's greatest collections of European paintings. Open Monday, Wednesday, Friday, Saturday 10:00 to 6:00; Tuesday and Thursday 10:00 to 9:00 p.m.; Sundays 2:00 to 6:00. The National Portrait Gallery (next door) boasts paintings, sculptures, and photographs of the famous by the famous. Open weekdays 10:00 to 5:00, Saturdays to 6:00, Sundays 2:00 to 6:00.

The Tate Gallery, overlooking the river in Westminster (Millbank, S.W.1), houses a national collection of British painting but also, more importantly for most overseas visitors, splendid collections of modern painting and sculpture from many lands. It is strong on Blake, Turner, the French Impressionists, and the pre-Raphaelites, and stages frequent shows of contemporary art. Open weekdays and Saturdays 10:00 to 6:00; Sundays 2:00 to 6:00. Free lectures.

The Wallace Collection (Manchester Square, in Marylebone) is made up preponderantly of French paintings of the 18th and 19th centuries, set among furniture, sculpture and porcelain of the same periods. Other Continental schools are represented (notably the later Venetians), and there is a vast amount of arms and armor. Weekdays 10:00 to 5:00, Sundays from 2:00.

The Courtauld Institute Galleries, in Woburn Square, W.C.1, house the important art collections which have been bequeathed to London University. The exhibits include a number of first-rate French Impressionist canvases and the Roger Fry Collection. The galleries are open six days a week from 10:00 to 5:00, and on Sundays from 2:00 to 5:00.

The Institute of Contemporary Arts (Nash House, The Mall, S.W. 1) exhibits recent art. Open Tuesdays through Saturdays 12:00 to 8:00, Sundays 2:00 to 8:00.

The Queen's Gallery, Buckingham Palace (Buckingham Palace Road, S.W. 1) is worth a visit for a look at masterpieces from the Royal Collection. Open Tuesdays through Saturdays 11:00 to 5:00, Sundays 2:00 to 5:00. (See also British Museum, page 40.)

The Hayward Gallery (Belvedere Road, S.E.1), the Whitechapel Art Gallery (Whitechapel High Street, E.1), and the American Embassy (Grosvenor Square) regularly put on shows, the last-named of American art. See the latest issue of *The Arts Review* (30 p.), every other Saturday, or the monthly *Art and Artists* (60 p.). The London Transport Authority publishes a useful booklet called *Museums and Art Galleries In and Near London* (free).

The Royal Societies present shows during "the season" (May–October) which are usually well advertised by posters in the Underground and elsewhere. These include the Royal Academy of Arts (Burlington House, Piccadilly, W.1), the Federation of British Artists with continuous exhibitions of all kinds of British art at the Mall Galleries (The Mall, S.W. 1).

The Strand is busy day or night

There is a vast open-air show of contemporary art staged annually, in August and September, in Heath Street, at the edge of Hampstead Heath (Underground: Hampstead). The quality of the work varies considerably, as in the open-air shows around New York's Washington Square.

Auctions. Art and art objects are among the commodities in the buying and selling of which London stands supreme. One reason is geographical (accessibility to Continental suppliers and purchasers); another, financial (sellers' commissions are low). Of the literally hundreds of auction rooms and houses in London in which this trade is constantly carried on, two are renowned the world over: Sotheby's, at 34 New Bond Street, W.1, and Christies, at 8 King Street, St. James's, S.W.1. Both handle paintings, prints, silver, jewelry, rare books, porcelain, carpets, antique furniture, etc. Sotheby's Belgravia, at 19 Motcomb Street, S.W. 1, auctions only Victoriana. Even if you have no intention of buying anything, these auctions are a London spectacle not to be missed. Special sales fetch enormous sums and make front-page news, but lesser sales—that you can probably afford—are going on all the time. Auctions, announced in the *Daily Telegraph* on Mondays and in the *Times* on Tuesdays, take place on weekday mornings at 11:00. Catalogues of upcoming sales are available for a few pennies, and anyone who wants to can attend.

The City at Work. Apropos of watching Londoners at work—a pleasant pastime when one is on vacation—there are many ways of doing this.

Any time between 10:00 and 3:15 on weekdays you can see (but not hear) the Stock Exchange in action. From the glassed-in gallery the black-suited traders on the floor below look like oversized ants, and their ceaseless surgings from this pillar to that post likewise resemble the purposeful activity of those insects. There is also a free film. The entrance is at Tower Block, Old Broad Street, E.C.2. (Underground: Bank).

Ships from all the world's ports line the London docks

Not far away, at Rosebery Avenue, E.C.1, is the Mount Pleasant station of the Post Office. There you can watch all the mail that comes into the country being sorted. Guides will show you around during the evenings, but you must write first to the Controller, Mount Pleasant, E.C.1.

More suggestions of this kind are given under various headings below.

Crafts and Design. Three places that are far too often overlooked by people who are not impelled to visit them for professional reasons are the British Craft Centre, the Crafts Advisory Committee and the Design Centre. The first, at 43 Earlham Street, W.C.2 (836-6993) exhibits and sells British craftsmanship in many fields such as silver, jewelry, metalwork, ceramics, woodwork, textiles, book-binding, and embroidery. It is open weekdays from 10:00 to 5:30, and Saturday mornings from 10:00 to 1:00.

The Crafts Advisory Committee, at 12 Waterloo Place, Lower Regent Street (839-8000) is part of the Design Council and has a different exhibition every two months as well as an index of British craftsmen with photographic slides of their work for you to use in choosing a work you might like to commission. The Committee does no direct selling.

The Design Centre, 28 Haymarket, S.W.1 (also part of the Design Council at 839-8000) features six-week exhibits of all that is best in modern design, displaying objects and photographs. Open Mondays through Saturdays from 9:30 to 5:30, with late opening until 9:00 p.m. on Wednesdays and Thursdays.

You might also like to visit the Craftsmen Potters Shop, William Blake House (his birthplace), Marshall Street, W.1 (437-7605) where the finest pots in Britain are displayed and sold. Open Monday through Friday, 10:00 to 5:30, Saturdays 10:30–1:00.

Free Speech. A frequently heard observation is that "you see England at its best at Marble Arch." Whether or not you agree, you certainly won't fail to find a visit to Speakers' Corner, at the northeast extremity of Hyde Park near "the Arch," stimulating, provocative, illuminating, entertaining or amusing—and quite possibly all of these. Here is the homeland of free speech, with impassioned orators trumpeting their beliefs regarding politics, religion, and many other subjects. Hecklers are there in plenty, but the crowds invariably uphold the speakers' right to say their piece. The best times for this great free show are late summer afternoons and evenings and Sunday after-

Dome of St. Paul's; Mary le Bow, Cheapside

repressible 18th-century liberal who fought as furiously as any man in England for the rights of the American colonists. Here, you may want to take a last look back at the magnificent, if grimy, façade of Wren's masterpiece. On the other side of Ludgate Circus is **Fleet Street**, the "Street of Ink," along which are concentrated the offices of newspapers whose combined readership exceeds the population of the United Kingdom and whose influence is felt daily all over the world. In front of **St. Dunstan's Church**, on the right-hand side, is a 1586 statute of the first Elizabeth, and the curious old clock whose attendant giants strike the quarter-hours with their clubs. On further are the **Law Courts**. Here, at the **Victorian Temple Bar Memorial**, familiarly known as "The Griffin," Fleet Street becomes the Strand, and the City of London meets the City of Westminster.

Before leaving the City, even the most hurried visitor should turn into **Middle Temple Lane**, opposite the Law Courts, and spend a few minutes strolling through the ancient quadrangles, lawns and gardens of the Temple, which Charles Lamb called "the most elegant spot in the metropolis." Originally the property of the Knights Templars, the Temple has been, since the 14th century, a school for lawyers, and in spite of extensive rebuilding necessitated by war damage, has retained its flavor of a university town, with associations dating from the time of the Crusades. The contrast it affords with busy Fleet Street is extraordinary. The **Temple Church**, belonging to both of the Temple Inns of Court (Middle Temple and Inner Temple), is one of the four remaining Norman "round" churches in England.

From the "Griffin" (at which point British monarchs must still obtain the Lord Mayor's formal permission before they may enter the City), you turn westward again and immediately confront a statue of Dr. Johnson, appropriately facing his beloved Fleet Street, and behind him his church, **St. Clement Danes**, situated on an "island" in the Strand. This is the "Oranges and lemons" church of the old song. Beyond it, on another "island," stands the church of **St. Mary-le-Strand**, with **Somerset House** to the left. This 18th-century public building houses the Probate Registry and the Register General; wills kept here date from 1382, and for a small fee you may examine any will, including those of Shakespeare, Johnson, William Penn, Nelson, Dickens and Florence Nightingale.

London Day by Day 37

noons all year 'round. In the City, you may find similar goings-on at Tower Hill; and on Hampstead Heath, at Whitestone Pond.

Occasionally, on Sunday afternoons, Trafalgar Square is the scene of mass meetings and demonstrations—most often as the climax of a protest march through the streets of London.

Fun... If you're fed up with sight-seeing and feel like relaxing, London has a fine amusement park in Battersea Park across the Thames from Chelsea. As this guidebook went to press, the park was undergoing a major overhaul and was closed to visitors. A magnificent Magic World—the English answer to Disneyland—is due to open there in late 1976 or early 1977. Interested visitors can get further information from the London Tourist Board.

... and Games. Perhaps your fancy calls for a bit of sport without any corresponding urge to work up a sweat. If so, why not try some of the games the British play? Most are quite simple and are played in pubs. While different establishments have different facilities, there is sure to be a place within a short walk of wherever you may be which offers one, at least, of the following popular pastimes:

Darts—a kind of bowless archery in which the players toss steel shafts encased in wooden jackets trimmed with feathers at a circular target mounted on a wall. Most pubs are equipped with darts and boards—just ask the publican (bartender).

Bar Billiards—a modified form of pool, played on a much smaller table. The object is to sink the balls without knocking over the wooden "toadstools." Less frequently encountered is Snooker—which *is* pool.

Shove Ha'penny—most popular in working-class districts such as the East End—used to be played with ha'pennies on a board or marked-out table-top. A 2 p. piece is used now.

Rarer than the foregoing are dominoes and checkers (which the British continue to call by the old name of draughts). In certain *raffiné* coffee bars, the owners will produce a chess set on demand. As in Paris, pinball machines have recently cropped up everywhere—sometimes in quite unlikely places.

Hyde Park, where free speech becomes an occupation and an entertainment

"Chemmy" parties, where you were expected to gamble fairly sizable amounts on *chemin de fer*, used to flourish illegally. In these enlightened times you may lose your money without the risk of being railroaded at various gambling clubs, all of which require the payment of membership fees. Under a new law they cannot be mentioned by name here, but taxi drivers and hotel clerks often can steer you to them. Cost of membership varies, but visitors can usually negotiate for a temporary membership for about £5 ($10.00).

Law. The Central Criminal Court, better known, after the street on which it stands, as the Old Bailey, is an excellent spot for watching the famous British judicial system in operation. Judges and learned counsel wear robes and wigs, and the bench is still furnished with bouquets on the opening days of sessions—used in the old days to mask the stench of the prisoners. Admission to the public gallery of all Courts (there are twelve new ones) is from 10:15 to 1:00, and from 1:45 to 4:30 every weekday. If the proceedings are really newsworthy—a murder case or a Liberace libel suit—you'll have to line up early to get a seat.

Rich in human interest and in items for the evening newspapers are the Magistrate's Courts. The best known of London's thirteen are those at Bow Street, W.C.2, just off Covent Garden and Marlborough Street, W.1. They are open from 10:00 to 5:00, with a break for lunch. The spicier offenses—those committed after dark—are dealt with the following morning.

Literature. Like the law, literature is a field of creative activity in which the English have managed to hold their own quite well, and London is consequently a literary mecca. Pilgrims in search of shrines and memorabilia relating to some favorite author will usually know where to go; if not, they can get specific information by dropping into any public library. Round blue plaques posted on house-fronts show who lived where, and when.

London is, of course, with New York, one of the two great centers of publishing in the English language. New books are constantly coming out and being reviewed, and new writers (and their critics) can be seen almost as constantly talking, arguing, drinking, and occasionally even writing, in the pubs and coffee bars of Chelsea, Soho, and Hampstead. For bookhunters, central London is a paradise, particularly in the Charing Cross Road area.

Markets. People who enjoy watching unrehearsed shows—not to mention hearing and smelling them—will find nothing in London quite so gratifyingly alive as the markets.

Portobello Road Market, whose shops and stalls are often closed during the week, is booming on Saturday mornings, and is *the* place to find absolutely everything from food to furniture, flowers, books and any category of junk, is in Notting Hill Gate, and stretches for a few miles, joining a more pedestrian market at Goldhawk Road, which is full of local color.

Camden Passage Market, in Islington, features antiques, stamps, coins, china, silver, bric a brac, and open market stalls on Wednesdays and Saturdays.

Billingsgate, just down-river from London Bridge, is the city's roughest, toughest market, which long ago gave its name to a particularly virulent form of verbal abuse. It is the fish capital of Britain. Trading begins at 6:00 A.M. and goes on until 9:00. The white-coated porters wear leather hats called billy-cocks which are said to be direct descendants of the helmets worn by English bowmen at the Battle of Agincourt. The flashing activity, the hoarse cries ("Eels!—Oh, lurvely! Fresh eels!") and the sight and smell of millions of fresh-caught sea fish add up to an impression that should stay with you a long time.

Borough Market, across London Bridge in Southwark, is quieter, but its fruits and vegetables display a greater color range than Billingsgate's fish. This is the Cockney's market, serving southeast London—the oldest part after the City.

The old and renowned Covent Garden Market, until late in 1974 just north of the Strand, was once the garden of a convent (hence the name), and later laid out as a piazza by Inigo Jones. For two centuries it was not only the leading market in England for fruit, flowers, and vegetables, but was also an integral part of the London theatrical scene. Eliza Doolittle sold flowers there, and generations of English authors and playwrights have immortalized the Market and its attendant features in their literary works. For today's visitor, there is *New* Covent Garden in Vauxhall, an outlying district of the city, which boasts 68 acres of modern facilities, including 45 acres of fruit and vegetables, and a three-acre temperature-controlled indoor flower market.

Leadenhall Market, in the City, occupies the site of the old Roman forum and deals in wholesale poultry and fish. Smithfield Market, off Farringdon Road in the City's northwest corner, is Britain's prime meat exchange; it was once a fair ground, the site of Bartholomew Fair, and at another time the place where Bloody Mary staged public executions. Spitalfields Market, in the East End, is a picturesque establishment for the buying and selling of vegetables.

Billingsgate, where the language and the produce come from

40 London

Museums. Markets are for early mornings in fine weather; at later hours, and particularly when it's raining, the museums of London can help you to pass an instructive hour or two. The great majority are free.

The British Museum boasts the Rosetta stone and the Elgin marbles from the Parthenon, among its enormous collection of antiquities, ethnography, and books. Its British Museum Library has hosted such readers as Virginia Woolf and Karl Marx. Off by itself in Bloomsbury (tube station: Russell Square or Tottenham Court Road). Open daily 10:00 to 5:00 and Sundays 2:30 to 6:00.

At Exhibition Road and the Cromwell Road (tube station: South Kensington, S.W. 7) are several first-rate museums: the Geological Museum; the Natural History Museum (dinosaur skeletons, 91-foot model whale); the Science Museum (working models activated by push buttons); and, last and most, the Victoria and Albert Museum (ornamental and applied art), the largest of the lot. All are open from 10:00 to 6:00 Monday through Saturday, 2:00 to 6:00 on Sundays. The Commonwealth Institute (life and resources of the British Commonwealth), a walk of several blocks north and west, closes somewhat earlier.

The Geffrye Museum, Kingsland Road, E.2 (Shoreditch), shows furniture dating from 1600 to the present in a series of sample rooms decorated with period pieces. Open weekdays 10:00–5:50, Sundays 2:00–5:50, closed Mondays.

The Imperial War Museum (1914 to the present), Lambeth Road, S.E.1, contains guns, tanks, and a complete visual record of two world wars. Weekdays 10:00–5:50, Sundays from 2:00 to 5:50. For military history before 1914, visit the National Army Museum, Royal Hospital Rd., Chelsea S.W.3. Weekdays 10:00–5:30, Sundays 2:00 to 5:30.

The Jewish Museum at Woburn House, Upper Woburn Place, W.C.1, has numerous fascinating relics of world Jewry. Monday through Thursday, 2:30–5:00, Friday and Sunday, 10:30–12:45, closed Saturday.

The British Museum

London Day by Day

The London Museum, Kensington Palace, W.8, is a museum of old London illustrated with plans, models, etc. Opens weekdays at 10:00, Sundays at 2:00; closes at 6:00 in summer, 5:00 in winter.

The Wellcome Museum of Medical Science, 183 Euston Road, N.W. 1, contains over 200,000 exhibits dealing with the history of medicine. Open 10:00–5:00 weekdays and Saturdays, closed Sundays.

The Wellington Museum, Apsley House, 149 Piccadilly, W.1, at Hyde Park Corner, was long known as "Number 1, London" in honor of its distinguished occupant, the Iron Duke, whose relics it houses. Included are three superb Velázquezes, the spoils of war, which Wellington was allowed to keep after Waterloo. Weekdays 10:00–6:00, Sunday 2:30–6:00.

Although it can hardly be classified as a museum, this is probably the best spot to discuss Madame Tussaud's Waxworks. This extraordinary show has been in existence over 200 years, and has been in business in London since 1802. Premises are near Baker Street Station, N.W.1, in Marylebone. The startlingly lifelike effigies of notable and notorious individuals have fascinated generations of Londoners, and are worth a visit for the accuracy of the costumes alone. Frequent additions are made to the collection, among them film stars, sports heroes, and contemporary American presidents. The Chamber of Horrors is guaranteed to give you a good, clean, morbid, thrill, and tell you something about the seamy side of London's past into the bargain. Open weekdays 10:00 to 5:30, closes at 6:30 Saturdays and Sundays. Admission 85 pence for adults, 45 pence for children.

Newspapers. Because Britain is geographically a small country, the daily and weekly newspapers published in and around Fleet Street are national rather than regional. This explains why none of them includes "London" in its name. It also accounts for their circulations, which are staggering by American standards, even by contrast with the New York *Daily News* or the Chicago *Tribune*.

With reference to the London press generally, you will probably be surprised by (a) the inordinate amount of space given over to gossip and chitchat, (b) the prominence accorded financial news, (c) the undisguised editorializing in the news columns. Features to look for are the political cartoons (best in the world); the book, drama, and movie reviews; and the crossword puzzles, utterly different from the American brand as the clues abound with puns, anagrams, and similar brain-teasers.

As everybody must surely know, *The Times* is in a class by itself. Once so conservative in its makeup that it printed only a mass of what the British call "small ads" on its front page instead of news (Kennedy's assassination being a very rare exception), *The Times* recently changed all that and now prints important news on the front page, sometimes even in the block capitals of far less distinguished newspapers. According to legend, *The Times* has an inside track with all British governments—particularly Conservative ones. Printed on high-quality paper, as befits the journal of record, it costs 10 p.

The *Daily Telegraph* is England's true middle-class newspaper: conservative in makeup, politics and outlook, it appeals to a readership of sound, respectable citizens possessed of tolerably high intelligence. The *Guardian,* long regarded in many quarters as the best newspaper in Britain and considered must reading for intellectuals, is liberal in outlook and Liberal in politics.

Unlike any of the journals mentioned so far, the *Express* shows not the slightest restraint in handling the news. It is unashamedly sensational and jingoistic, following a right-wing line and grinding the ax, not of any party but of its proprietor, Sir Max Aitken. Beside it, its leading competitor, the Conservative *Daily Mail,* seems a pale imitation. The difference between the two is aptly summarized by the difference between the emblem of the first (a battle-bound Crusader, printed in red) and the pious motto of the second—"For Queen and Commonwealth."

The *Sun* is strongly left-wing, and closely follows the workings of the Unions. The *Morning Star* is the official organ of the British Communist Party.

In addition to the foregoing, London has two afternoon papers: the *Evening News* and the *Standard.* Each is allied with a big morning daily. The *Evening News* is, like the *Daily Mail,* Conservative and popular. The *Standard* is a bit sensationalist, excellent for gossip, and a bit pretentious as well. Its art, film, and theatre reviews are quite reliable—its literary and show business gossip may be less so. The *Standard* is considered *the* paper for apartment-hunting. Both the *Evening News* and the *Standard* have seven daily editions, the evening ones being the most useful for visitors.

Dailies cost from 6 p. to 10 p.

Band of the Grenadier Guards

The *U* weekly papers are the *Sunday Times* (no connection with *The Times*), the *Sunday Telegraph,* and the *Observer*. The first two are conservative, the third liberal, and all are crammed with worthwhile articles and reviews. The three have hard-working and fair-minded reporters in the United States.

After these, the deluge—of strictly *non-U* mass entertainment, carefully designed to titillate the British family relaxing at home on its one full day off, with feet up and collars unbuttoned. The fare served up is richly spiced with shocks and scandals. Papers in this category include the *Sunday Mirror*, the *People*, and the *Sunday Express.* Finally, there is the *News of the World*, whose circulation of six million plus, while down from a peak of eight million, makes it far and away the most widely read newspaper on earth.

Pageantry I: Daily. Some of the best shows put on in London are entirely free. These are the traditional ceremonies. Continuously re-enacted, they serve to remind Londoners of their heritage and rarely fail to impress even the most blasé of visitors from overseas—perhaps because the participants take their roles so seriously, and play them without any trace of self-consciousness. Anachronistic they may be, yet the angriest young Englishman is hard put not to be affected by them. We Americans, on the other hand, can enjoy them for the colorful spectacles they are, without necessarily becoming emotionally involved.

The Changing of the Guard takes place daily throughout the year (in winter it may be only once every two days) at 11:30 A.M., unless otherwise stated in the press or on the radio. The Guards wear full dress, i.e. red jackets, during summer, usually April 1 to September 30, when they begin using their long grey winter coats, unless the weather is still warm at the customary time of changeover. The new guard assembles in Chelsea or Wellington Barracks, and the troops march behind a band to the forecourt of the Palace. A traditional march is played as the keys are given over to the new Guard. Sometimes the ceremony takes place at St. James's Palace. In very bad weather, the full ceremony outside Buckingham Palace is considerably shortened. For the latest information call 930-4466.

The Changing of the Queen's Life Guard, also called "Mounting the Guard," is the public's second most favorite military ceremony. It takes place daily at 11:00 and an hour earlier on Sundays at the Horse Guards Arch, Whitehall, S.W. 1. The old guard, in its fine Household Cavalry uniform, is relieved by the new. The new guard rides from the Knightsbridge Barracks via the Mall. The guard crosses Horse Guards Parade.

Springtime at Regents Park

The oldest ritual of all takes place between 9:53 and 10:00 at night. This is the ceremonial locking up of the Tower of London, known as the Ceremony of the Keys. At about 9:40 a Yeoman Warder starts rattling off an explanation of the activities to come; when it's over, you and your party are shepherded to the Bloody Tower, where four guardsmen stand waiting to escort the keys. By the light of an ancient lantern, the chief warder marches his men to the entrance and to the gates of the various towers, locking each in turn. At the Bloody Tower the sentry challenges the detail, and a formal exchange ensues: "Halt!" "Detail halt." "Who goes there?" "Keys." "Whose Keys?" "Queen Elizabeth's Keys." "Advance Queen Elizabeth's Keys. All's well." The final phase of the ceremony consists of military maneuvers perfectly timed so that just before the clock strikes ten and the bugler blows the Last Post, the chief warder has intoned "God preserve Queen Elizabeth" and the others have chorused a solemn "Amen."

This ceremony, like the others, is free, but unfortunately can be witnessed by only a limited number at a time. You must apply in writing to the Resident Governor, giving a preferred date and an alternative one, and stating how many people you want to bring along.

Pageants II: Annual. If you happen to be in London when one of the major annual ceremonies is being enacted, you should try not to miss it. The following is a short list, in chronological order.

Trooping the Colour takes place on the monarch's official birthday, the first or second Saturday in June. (The Queen's actual birthday is April 21.) This is the height of military pomp, dating back to ancient times. It can be viewed from any point between Horse Guards Parade and Buckingham Palace.

The "Watermen's Derby" on August 1, is a rowing race among Thames watermen. The course is from London Bridge to Cadogan Pier (at the Albert Bridge, by Cheyne Walk, in Chelsea)—a distance of 4½ miles. The coveted first prize, bestowed originally in 1715 by one Thomas Doggett, is a "Coat of Orange Livery" and a silver badge. Other prizes include a pair of breeches and £20.

A colorful legal procession occurs in mid-October, when Her Majesty's Judges and Queen's Counsel have breakfast with their chief, the Lord Chancellor, at the House of Lords. After this, they file solemnly to Westminster Abbey for a special service—the judges in ermine and scarlet, the Q.C.s in silk gowns, and all in full-bottomed wigs.

In late October or early November—or shortly after a General Election—comes the State Opening of Parliament. To the tumultuous applause of her subjects, the Queen is driven in the Irish State Coach, with a royal escort, from Buckingham Palace to the House of Lords. A royal salute is fired in St. James's Park.

November 5, the anniversary of the Gunpowder Plot of 1605, in which Guy Fawkes and his fellow conspirators allegedly came within an ace of blowing up Parliament, is marked by no official pageantry. For weeks before the date, however, small fry trundle homemade effigies of Mr. Fawkes in baby carriages through the streets, imploring "A penny for the Guy." On the fifth—and the days preceding it—they have a riotous good time harrying their elders by exploding ear-shattering fireworks bought with the proceeds of their begging.

A few days after this, on a Saturday early in November, comes the City's traditional spectacle, the Lord Mayor's Show. This ceremony goes back to the 16th century, when the newly elected Lord Mayor of London went in style to Westminster, attended by the "crafts in their best liveries" to present himself to the monarch. Nowadays, the new Lord Mayor is driven in his ornate and ponderous state coach (built in 1757) to the Law Courts, where he is received by the Lord Chief Justice as the Queen's representative. This is, historically, the City's favorite show.

Parks. The favorite *permanent* show of most Londoners is probably the flora and fauna of their city's parks. William Pitt the Elder used to speak of the parks as "the lungs of London," and the description is, if anything, more apt today than when it was coined. Certainly no other feature contributes more to the "livability" of the British capital.

Visitors are frequently surprised to discover how much of the metropolis is covered by parkland. Greater London is ringed by a wide Green Belt, in which construction is prohibited, and in the West End itself it is possible to stroll for three miles without encountering traffic or built-up areas for more than a minute or two on the way. Starting at Westminster, the route lies through St. James's Park, Green Park, Hyde Park, and Kensington Gardens.

The 93 acres of St. James's Park were swampy meadowland until Henry VIII drained them to make a nursery for the royal deer. Charles II, who was very fond of the spot, introduced ducks and, as Pepys noted, "a great variety of water fowl." Today the islands of the lake are bird sanctuaries. The park was laid out almost in its present form in 1825 by the great architect Nash. The view from the ornamental bridge is said to be the finest in London, but it attracts less attention than the weird antics of the comical pelicans.

Green Park (53 acres), added by the Merry Monarch, is a restful, tree-studded grassland surrounded by some of London's busiest thoroughfares, including Piccadilly. Sheep, pastured there from time to time, heighten the illusion of being deep in the country.

Such illusions can be even more real in 360-acre Hyde Park, Henry VIII's hunting grounds, where wild rabbits scamper about and where a bird sanctuary, adorned with the late Jacob Epstein's *Rima*, expresses the love of nature of W. H. Hudson, author of *Green Mansions*, to whose memory the controversial sculpture is dedicated. The Serpentine, a lovely artificial lake, is popular for both rowing and swimming, and Rotten Row (*Route du Roi*), the broad, mile-and-a-half-long track which was the scene of so many romantic encounters between well-born gentlemen and ladies in Victorian and Edwardian times, is the favorite bridle path of London's riders. But a great deal of the park is simply natural scenery—a haven of peace and quiet.

Kensington Gardens (275 acres), the western extension of Hyde Park, likewise seems strangely remote, in places, from streets and shops. Its famous statue of Peter Pan occupies a special place in the affections of Kensington's many "nannies," not to mention their former charges.

Four-hundred-twenty-seven-acre Regent's Park, to the north, was once, like Hyde Park, a royal hunting ground. Early in the last century it was laid out by Nash on the orders of the Prince Regent, and today it is the most complete of London's parks, with everything a park ought to have. There is a big lake for grownups to go rowing on and a pond for children, a magnificent rose and rock garden, playing fields, a running track, and an open-air theatre. The Londoners' favorite zoo occupies the north side of Regent's Park. This internationally famous institution houses a wild animal population of over 10,000. It has a magnificent aquarium, and there is an extraordinary aviary designed by Lord Snowdon; the spectator walks over a narrow ramp, suspended above a waterfall, in the very midst of the exotic birds.

Hampstead Heath, still farther north, is mostly wild heathland, with green hills, wooded dells, and shaded waters—820 acres of lovely, unspoiled countryside. The highest point along Spaniards Road (440 feet) offers a superb panoramic vista of London, with the hills of Kent and Surrey forming the backdrop to St. Paul's and the Houses of Parliament. Adjoining the Heath are the 195-acre grounds of Ken Wood.

These, with Battersea Park, are the major parks of central London. For the sake of completeness, a few others farther out must be mentioned. Near Hampton Court Park stretches 1,099-acre Bushy Park. Richmond Park (2,358 acres) is the biggest in Greater

London maintained by the Government. The Royal Botanic Gardens at Kew, close by, are the most famous in the world. In south London are Blackheath Common and Greenwich Park; to the east lie Hainault Forest (1,108 acres) and Victoria Park, the "Hyde Park of the East End." Epping Forest, to the northeast, is by far the biggest open space, comprising 6,000 acres in Greater London alone.

Sports I: for Participants. In addition to the outdoor activities mentioned above under "Parks," there are plenty of other opportunities open to the visiting sportsman. In or near London you can play golf or tennis, swim, go bowling, sailing, or motorboating, fly a plane or (as implied) get a horse.

Within a fifty-mile radius of Charing Cross there are over 260 golf courses. Visitors are welcome at almost all private clubs on weekdays; it's advisable, though, to contact the secretary before turning up. For up-to-date information consult "Where to Golf" in *Golf International* (25 p.) every Friday.

Nearly all of London's large parks have public tennis courts which can be booked during working hours simply by going to the park keeper's office. The charges are low.

London also has many excellent indoor swimming pools. The best are at Swiss Cottage (278-4444), Chelsea Manor St., S.W.3 (352-6985) and Marshall St., S.W.1 (437-7665).

Sports II: for Spectators. As you might suppose, London is the sports capital of Britain. For some sports it is the world capital. Lord's Cricket Ground is the international home of cricket; the Oxford-Cambridge boat race on the Thames (late March or early April) is the oldest rowing event in existence; and Wimbledon (where the international tournament takes place in the last week of June) outranks even Forest Hills in the world of amateur tennis.

A glance at any newspaper reveals that the traditional British passion for sports continues undiminished. Almost every day of the year you can take your pick of a number of sports spectacles. For what's on, see *This Month in London* each month.

Cricket. Unless you hail from the Philadelphia Main Line, you've probably never seen this leisurely national rite being performed. Why not discover what it's all about at Lord's, in St. John's Wood, or at Kennington Oval in south Lambeth? Matches are played at both places nearly every day from May through early September; they last two or three days (play from 11:30 to 6:00). Ticket information can be had by calling either place—289-1615 or 735-2424. Oxford *vs.* Cambridge and Eton *vs.* Harrow at Lord's (early July), and if the touring international teams are in England, Test matches at Lord's (last week of June) and "the Oval" (third week of August).

Football is, of course, what we call soccer (derived from "association" in "association football"). It draws gigantic crowds to mammoth stadia, and the season extends through fall, winter and spring, culminating in the Cup Final at Wembley in late April or early May.

"All My Own Work"—pavement artists are a London institution

Games are played on Saturday afternoons. See any newspaper for forthcoming games.

Greyhound Racing is enormously popular. Meetings usually begin at 7:15 or 7:30 P.M., with eight races at half-hour intervals. Under the floodlights the crowd seems to go mad with excitement, and Saturday night is the looniest night of the week. There are tracks at Catford, Charlton, Clapton, Hackney Wick, Harringay, Hendon, Romford, Wembley, West Ham, White City, and Wimbledon. For details, consult the early editions of the evening papers.

Horse Racing may be the sport of kings (and queens), but it attracts less exalted members of the community as well. The scene at the track is often highly picturesque, what with the bookies and their tote boards, the gypsies, the toffs in their finery, and the sinister-looking types out of an English Damon Runyon. The big social events are Ascot Week (early June) and Goodwood (late July). The Derby (with a broad "a"), run at Epsom in June, is possibly the best and certainly the best-known horse race in the world. All three of these courses are within easy reach of London and are devoted exclusively to flat-racing (season, March to November). Steeplechasing goes on throughout the year except in high summer. London race courses are: Kempton Park, Sunbury (Middlesex); and in Surrey,

Sandown Park, Esher; and Epsom. Consult *Sporting Life* (12 p.) every day, for meetings.

Street Entertainers. Two products of London's rich imagination for which you should keep an eye and an ear out, are the sidewalk artists and the street musicians. Both species are peripatetic. The first, whose boast of "All My Own Work" seems a trifle superfluous, draw pictures in colored chalk on the pavement, leaving a cap or open cigar box out front for contributions. Be careful not to step on the view of Windsor Castle at Sunrise. These works and their creators can sometimes be found (in fair weather) in much-frequented places like Hyde Park Corner, the entrance to Green Park Underground, Shaftesbury Avenue at Cambridge Circus, and Trafalgar Square.

Street musicians, singly or in pairs, are called *buskers,* and can always be found wherever there's a crowd, playing a wide range of instruments and tunes; buskers perform for theatre lines, and are often on Shaftesbury Avenue and in Leicester Square. Watch for the Happer Wonderers, an old-time brass band made up of old-timers in uniform. Their wide repertoire includes familiar music-hall numbers and popular favorites, and they have lately taken with gusto to Dixieland.

USEFUL TIPS

Public Telephones. Using a public telephone in England used to be a considerable ordeal for the foreigner, because of complicated equipment and instructions. The system is very simple if you remember to dial your number first, wait until someone answers, and *then* push a 2-penny coin into the appropriate slot. (You will hear a loud buzzing noise, called "pips," until the money is deposited. At the end of four minutes (for central London) the pips will begin again, and you will have to put in more money. 10 p. pieces can be deposited for long distance calls or long city calls. There are different area codes for different sections of the country; the code for London is 01, to be used only when calling the city from elsewhere in the country.

Medical Care and Drugs. If you fall sick, your hotel or landlady can put you in touch with a doctor, or vice versa. If you specify that you want treatment on the National Health Scheme (available to overseas visitors just as it is to the British who pay for it with weekly contributions), it will cost you next to nothing. However you won't have much say about who treats you and hospital accommodations will not be luxurious. The same goes for dental treatment. Prescriptions can be filled at any drugstore (chemist's shop). The *Boots the Chemists* outlet in Piccadilly Circus is open all night, every night. Bliss, 54 Willesden Lane, N.W. 6, is also open all night.

Mounted Life Guards at Hyde Park

If you get lost, any bobby will direct you. To report a fire, a crime or an accident, dial 999 from any telephone (no pennies needed). And if you are overcome by homesickness, you can go to the magnificent American Embassy in Grosvenor Square by day or drop into an American movie, just about anywhere in town, at other times.

One minor drawback in London (not so minor when needed) is the shortage of public rest rooms. Restaurants are not required to have them. Pubs are, but these may be closed, and there are not nearly enough municipal "conveniences," particularly for women. It's as well to bear this in mind and act accordingly.

Money. For centuries the British currency system, ignoring the decimal system in use throughout the major part of the world, mystified foreign visitors with its shillings, florins, half crowns, pounds and guineas. As of February, 1971, however, the British finally adopted a decimal system of their own. The pound, written £, is still in use, but instead of being made up of twenty shillings, it is now made up of one hundred new pence, written p.

Coins are minted in the denominations listed below; their dollar equivalents were valid when this book went to press.

$\frac{1}{2}$p.	called a half new penny	worth	1¢
1p.	" one " "	"	2¢
2p.	" two new pence	"	4¢
5p.	" five " "	"	10¢
10p.	" ten " "	"	20¢
50p.	" fifty " "	"	$1.00

There are bills in the following denominations: £1 ($2.00), £5 ($10.00), £10 ($20.00), £20 ($40.00).

One pound plus seventy-five new pence would be written as follows: £1.75, and in American dollars it would be worth $3.50.

Tipping practices in London are pretty much like those in the United States—15 per cent in restaurants and taxis, a little more in night clubs. For small-change tips, such as those you might give a hat-check girl or a hotel doorman, a convenient way to handle it is to use 5 new pence as you would a dime and 10 new pence as you would a quarter.

GETTING AROUND—TRANSPORTATION

Moving about in London is not difficult. Indeed, from most points of view, London is better served by its public and private transport (and its policemen and ordinary citizens, always ready to help a stranger out with directions) than is any other major city. Knowing how to make use of these services can save you many precious minutes, not to mention frayed nerves, aching feet, and money.

An alertness to the basic facts of London's traffic can even save your life. Everybody *knows*, for instance, that the British perversely insist on driving on the "wrong" side of the road, but acting on this knowledge is another matter. To do so, a person has to break the habits of a lifetime, and few of us find this easy. The result is that when you hear the sudden heart-stopping screech of tires on asphalt anywhere in central London, the chances are that some unwary foreigner on foot has glanced left, and then, seeing a deserted lane stretching invitingly away, stepped off the curb smack into the path of an onrushing car, truck, or bus. Astonishingly enough, no matter how frequently this incident is repeated, it practically never seems to end disastrously for the visitor, though it probably does little to endear him to local motorists.

Taxis. Since taxis possess obvious advantages for the visitor who hasn't yet got his bearings, we may logically take them up first before considering cheaper forms of transportation. The initial charge is 25 new pence for the first three-fifths of a mile. There is an additional charge of nine pence after midnight. There are also small extra charges for luggage carried outside, and for dogs—though this last is often overlooked in animal-loving England. Up to six miles, the meter dictates the fare, but beyond that distance, the amount payable is a matter for prior agreement between driver and passenger. A complete table of fares, charges, and conditions is posted in the back. As for tips, 7p. is the absolute minimum, for rides costing 30p. or less; above that figure, it is wise to add at least 2p. for every 10p. or fraction thereof showing on the meter.

After midnight, subway trains and most buses (except for the special night buses) have stopped running in most parts of London, and the only convenient way to get to your next port of call or your hotel will be by taxi. Unless there happens to be a taxi rank just outside the place where you are, or cabs dropping people off, your best bet will be to summon a cab by telephone rather than look for one in the street. You may call either a nearby cab rank or one of the radio-cab services; if you happen to be in a restaurant or a night club, someone on the staff will probably do this for you, but a good number to keep handy, for taxis anywhere in London and around the clock, is 286-4848. You will be asked your name, present address, and destination, and told how soon the cab will pick you up. Barring a sudden downpour at a busy hour, it should appear within minutes.

London cab drivers are certainly not all pillars of rectitude, but it can be confidently stated that they are fully as honest as their American counterparts. A "they're-out-to-fleece-me" attitude is nearly always unwarranted (and always disagreeable). If a disagreement should arise, the driver will be courteous, knowing that if he isn't, you may report him, by his brief and easy-to-remember license number, to the police. Unless you *know* he's in the wrong, it's therefore advisable to take his word for it—not simply for the sake of Anglo-American relations but because, in all probability, he is right.

The Tube. Next to taxis, the London subway system (officially, the Underground, unofficially, the Tube) offers the simplest and quickest means of proceeding from A to B. From most A's to most B's, that is. And the cash saving is considerable.

Of course you don't see much of the city traveling this way, but for many tourists this disadvantage is more than offset by the opportunity it affords to observe Londoners close up—discreetly, of course—even to the extent of (inadvertently) listening in on their conversations. In some respects the Underground is a better place in which to take the measure of London's extraordinarily varied population than any other, for here all classes mingle, as they do not, by and large, in specific bars and restaurants and other public places.

To urban Americans used to the drab discomfort of subway travel in cities like New York and Chicago, the relative luxuriousness of the London system comes as a delightful surprise. All the major stations are equipped with escalators (on which, incidentally, the unwritten rule is that you stand on the right, leaving an open lane on the left by which impatient travelers can hurry up or down), and practically all the others have elevators. Smoking is permitted everywhere, except in the cars displaying a "No Smoking" sign on their windows. Trains are frequent, fast, and clean. All in all, a ride on the Underground can be a very agreeable experience—though not, to be sure, during the rush hours. If, however, you should find yourself bucking the crowd at such times, you will probably be impressed by the good-humored patience that prevails among your fellow passengers.

The price you pay depends on how far you are going, most trips in central London and the areas immediately adjacent to it costing between 5p. and 20p. You buy a ticket (at the ticket window or at the coin machines) bearing the name of the station at which you are boarding your train, and surrender it at the end of your journey.

Unquestionably the main reason why more tourists don't make use of London's superb Underground is simply that they are afraid of getting lost. Considering the city's great size, and the complexity of its street layout, this fear is understandable. It is not, however, justified, for large schematic plans of the system are posted conspicuously in the stations, with the name of each stop printed in bold letters and the course of each of the seven component lines clearly indicated in its own distinctive color. Once aboard your train you will find a plan of the line along which you are traveling to remind you where to change—that is, if your trip necessitates changing. Altogether, it's difficult to imagine how a simpler system could possibly have been devised to handle the daily transportation of millions of Londoners along thousands of miles of track.

The Buses. How is one to sum up, in mere words, the lumbering pomp and magnificence of those wheeled leviathans, the world-renowned London omnibuses? These lordly double-deckers, painted a dazzling red, so dominate the street scene that they have virtually become the symbol or trademark of London. Wherever you go, there is sure to be one somewhere in sight—unless, of course, you happen to be waiting for one at a bus stop.

Quite apart from the superior sight-seeing a seat "on top" provides, a bus trip can, like a trip in the Underground, give you valuable insights into the character of London's people. The conductors, male and female, are themselves interesting examples of the species. Many are true-blue Cockney, but of recent years their ranks have been swollen by an influx of fresh talent from faraway Commonwealth countries like India and Jamaica. When the conductor approaches with a cry of, "Any more fares, please?" you simply tell him where you are going, and he will tell you the fare in pennies; pay him, and he will hand you in exchange a slip of paper which he cranks noisily out of the dispensing machine attached to his belt. It's a good idea to hold onto this ticket in case an inspector gets aboard. Contacts between bus conductors and the riding public are singularly breezy; when he takes your coins, the conductor will normally say "Ta"—Cockney for "Thank you"—and if *he* happens to be *she* (a "clippie" in London slang), you must not be surprised to hear yourself cozily addressed as "Love," "Ducks" or "Dearie"!

Car Hire. It is easy to rent a car, either to drive yourself around London or to be driven by a chauffeur. You can do this through your hotel, or through travel agencies like the American Express or Thomas Cook, or directly from Hertz (call 876-0484 for your nearest of 16 branches) or Avis (848-8733 for your nearest of 10). Costs are

54 London

from $8 to $50 a day plus mileage and gasoline. Costs are proportionately less by the week, and ten to fifteen per cent less off season. Your American license will suffice. Chauffeur-driven cars can be hired for approximately £60 ($120) plus tax for a 3-4 passenger car for 8 hours and 140 miles. Daily rate in London is £36 ($72.00) for 8 hours and 40 miles.

Conducted Tours. While American Express, Thomas Cook, and Universal Tours, among others, offer interesting tours of London during the summer (for times and prices you should consult the companies concerned, as these are subject to variation), the best and biggest bargain in this field is unquestionably London Transport's two-hour, twenty-mile tour, by double-decker bus, of the City and the West End. Buses leave Buckingham Palace Rd. (near Victoria) on the hour from 10:00 A.M. to 9:00 P.M. The all-inclusive price is 95p. (about $1.90) and children pay 60p. (about sixty cents less). London Transport also offers a tour of the City, one of Greenwich, one of Westminster, and one to Windsor and Hampton Court. Call 222-1234 for times and cost.

There are numerous other coach tours offered at very reasonable cost—to stately homes and other historic places near London. For information go to National Travel Ltd., Victoria Coach Station, Buckingham Palace Road, S.W. 1 (730-0202).

By Water. Every twenty minutes from 10:20 A.M. to dusk during the summer, a passenger launch departs from Westminster Pier (call 930-2074 for details) beneath the statue of Boadicea, and proceeds down the Thames to Greenwich, with a guide pointing out the attractions on either bank.

St. Paul's Cathedral, the heart of London before it was flanked by skyscrapers.

This two-hour round trip, which costing one pound, is a particularly painless way of absorbing a great deal of London scenery and history. Other boats run to Tower Bridge and back, stopping at the Tower of London, and still others run upstream to Putney, Hammersmith, Kew, Richmond, Kingston and Hampton Court. On all trips the fare is half for children under fifteen.

Last Notes on Navigation. You should have no difficulty locating the main attractions and points of interest in London, and if you do, anyone can direct you to them. But once you start exploring the city in greater detail, you will discover why so many English people, including those born and bred there, are to be seen consulting dog-eared atlases of London.

As if London's geography were not made confusing enough by the sheer number and planlessness of its components, the difficulties faced by a newcomer finding his way around are further compounded by local customs concerning the naming of streets, squares, and the like. Being nothing if not tradition-minded, the English are loath to discard a long-cherished name simply because it has ceased to bear any relation to the place it is supposed to describe. London Wall, Long Acre, Piccadilly, and Poultry may all be, in actual fact, public thoroughfares, but it would never occur to a Londoner to append "Street" or "Avenue" to their historic titles. And as the city has become more concentrated, spreading outward at the same time, not a few rustic-sounding "Walks," "Lanes," and "Roads," have been turned into busy metropolitan traffic arteries.

The terms "Gardens" and "Square" can be misleading, too, as by London usage they sometimes refer to open spaces entirely enclosed by buildings and having no relation other than proximity to the urban streets which bear the name.

Most streets follow the familiar system of house-numbering—even numbers on one side, odd on the other—but in some the numbers run in sequence down one side and up the other—why, no one can say. A few addresses do not refer to streets at all. Take, for example, "22 Pelham Court, S.W.3." You will search in vain for any such street, square, or even court, but a taxi driver or postman will know at once that the number signifies Flat No. 22 of an apartment building ("block of flats") of that name, at 145 Fulham Road, whither he will take you or your letter without hesitation.

On the whole, Londoners are well aware that foreigners find these quite mad, and are often inclined to agree. Whether they do or not, however, they will usually be happy to point out your way, perhaps throwing in a historical footnote, apocryphal or otherwise.

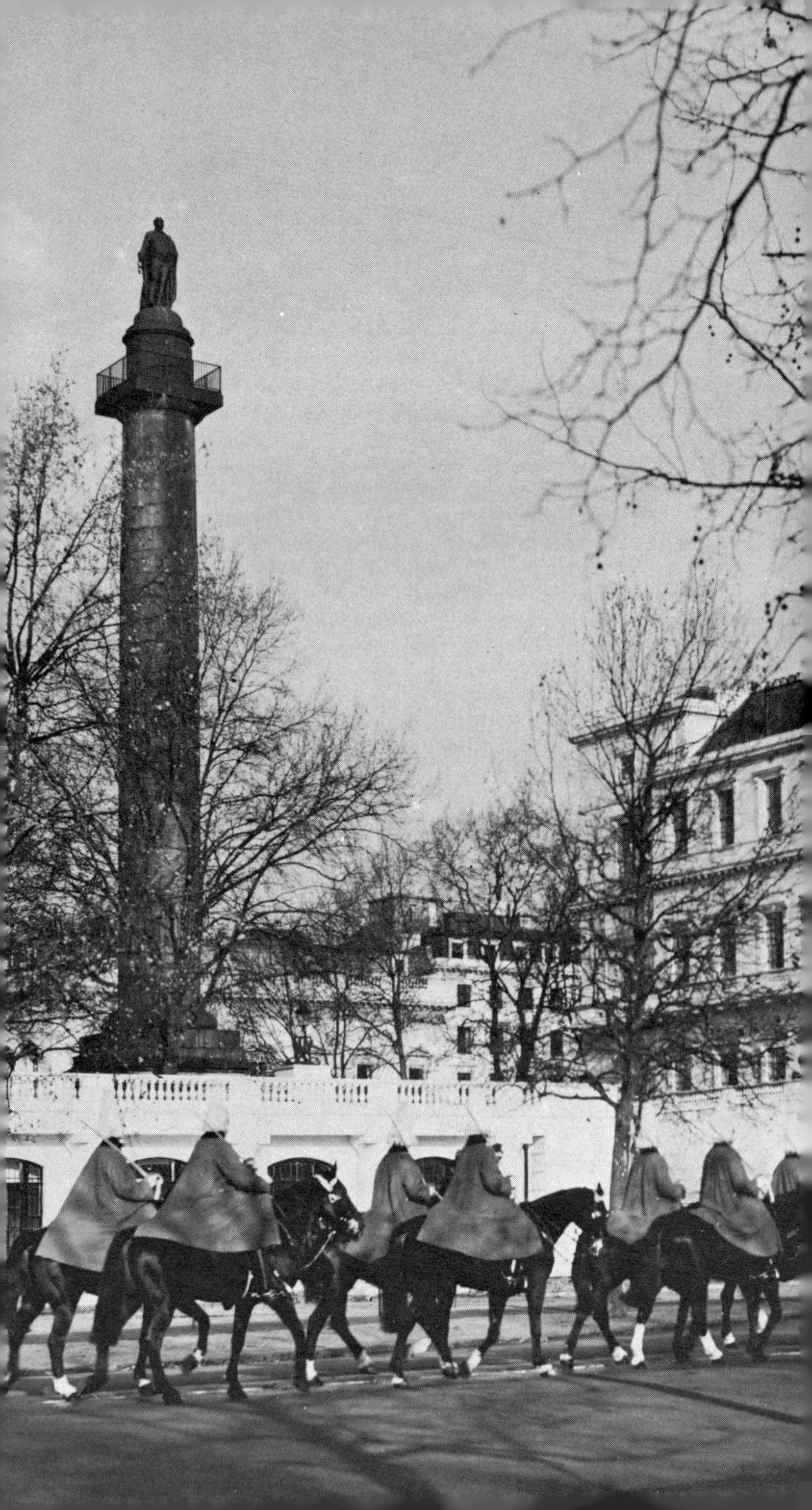

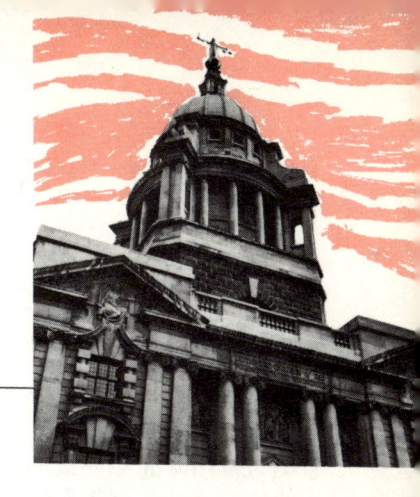

CHAPTER 5

HISTORIC LONDON

This chapter is a guide to the past; it deals with *historic* London. In order to help you plan your itinerary, the places you will want to see are listed geographically rather than alphabetically. The tour takes you from the Tower of London to St. Paul's Cathedral and on to Westminster Abbey. If you can spare only a few hours for old London, you had better confine yourself to the "musts" mentioned under separate headings. But if you have more time, it will be well spent investigating some of the historic buildings and monuments lining the route that links the "must" places. Brief descriptions are given in the text, and the places in this second category are indicated in boldface type. For visitors who can manage a leisurely exploration, the last four pages of the chapter cover other noteworthy sights in and outside of central London.

"Had we but world enough and time"—to quote Andrew Marvell—we might devote months or even years to a fascinating chronological excursion, commencing before the birth of Christ and extending to the present. After viewing the pre-Roman relics in the London and Guildhall Museums, we might proceed to Cannon Street, in the City, to inspect the ancient London Stone, the *lapis milliaris* which stood in the Roman Forum of Agricola, and from which distances were measured to other points in the colony of Britain. Next we would perhaps trace the direction of the old wall by means of the sections that survive—most notably, the bastion in the churchyard of St. Giles, Cripplegate. After that . . . But let's face it: none of us has that much "world" and "time." You will therefore probably want to head

The Life Guards in the Mall, below Wellington's Monument

straight for the city's most celebrated old architectural phenomenon, the venerable and formidable Tower of London.

THE TOWER OF LONDON

This medieval fortress, the most perfect in all England, is actually not one, but several buildings, comprising, with their grounds, a "liberty," which right is still asserted every three years in the ceremony of "beating the bounds." It stands not within the City but just east of it, and houses a self-contained community with its own rulers (the nonresident Constables of the Tower and the Resident Governor), chaplain, medical officer and coroner. Altogether, between 700 and 800 people live in "Her Majesty's Royal Fortress and Palace of the Tower of London," which explains why some parts are closed to the public. This population includes the infantry regiment stationed there, and of course the world-famous Yeomen Warders of the Tower, retired warrant officers and noncommisioned officers with excellent Army records, whose picturesque red, black, and gold Tudor uniforms are one of the main attractions of the place. Thirty-seven of these men—who are not to be confused with the "Beefeaters," the Yeomen of the Guard, whose uniforms are almost identical—are on duty during the day; they will be glad to show you around and tell you about the dramas that have been enacted behind these old stones.

At the center of the enclave stands its oldest and finest building, the **White Tower**, begun under William the Conqueror and slowly completed under his son, William Rufus. This is the "keep" of the fortress. Enclosing the spacious Inner Ward is a hexagonal wall from which rise thirteen towers, the best-known being the **Wakefield Tower** and the **Bloody Tower**, facing the river. Surrounding all this are fortifications, and around those, parade grounds and lawns which were, until 1843, a deep moat.

Today, the Tower still fulfills two of its original functions: fortress and treasury. Troops are garrisoned there, and the Crown Jewels are stored in the Wakefield Tower, where they may be seen for a small charge. In its time, however, the Tower has served many other uses. It was a royal palace until the time of James I, an observatory until the one at Greenwich was built in 1675, a mint until the nearby Royal Mint was built in 1810, a prison until 1820, and for five centuries, until 1834, the site of a royal menagerie. But it is chiefly as a prison that the Tower has imprinted itself—in the blackest hues—on the popular imagination. Its prisoners have included kings of Scotland, France, and England; queens, princes, and pretenders; and a great number of noblemen at odds with their sovereign, most of whom left the Tower only to walk to the headman's block on Tower Hill.

Much of the Tower is grim, in associations if not appearance: **Traitor's Gate**; the ghastly array of instruments of torture and exe-

Historic London

cution in the White Tower; and the Bloody Tower, where the "Little Princes" (Edward V and his brother the Duke of York) were done to death by order of their ambitious uncle the Duke of Gloucester (Richard III). There are the chambers in which Sir Walter Raleigh put in a total of eighteen comparatively easy years receiving his friends, conducting experiments in chemistry and writing *The History of the World;* and others where the pitiful sentiments of condemned men, carved by them in the woodwork, can still be deciphered. There is the spot where two of Henry VIII's queens were beheaded, and where the pathetic tragedy of Lady Jane Grey, nine days a queen, was brought to an end. There is the little church of **St. Peter ad Vincula** (in Chains), where many noble victims of the headman's ax lie buried. Of this place, Macauley wrote: "In truth, there is no sadder spot on earth than this little cemetery. Death is there associated, not, as in Westminster Abbey and St. Paul's, with genius and virtue, with public veneration and with imperishable renown; ... but with whatever is darkest in human nature and in human destiny, with the savage triumph of implacable enemies, with the inconstancy, the ingratitude, the cowardice of friends, with all the miseries of fallen greatness and of blighted fame."

But there are also at the Tower the exquisite Norman chapel of **St. John the Evangelist**, in the White Tower, and the magnificent display of the world's richest royal regalia (including an uncut ruby sent to the Black Prince by Pedro of Castile and the fabulous Koh-i-noor and Cullinan diamonds). There is a superb collection of arms and armor. And there is the unforgettable vision of the White Tower rising austere, but beautiful, from Tower Green, where Yeomen Warders pass, bearing their halberds, and tame ravens hop playfully about where so much savage tragedy has taken place.

A QUICK LOOK AT THE CITY

After seeing the Tower, the facts of geography combine neatly with those of history to suggest that instead of heading straight for St. Paul's, you stop first at the **Monument**, on Fish Street Hill, on the way. The Monument, a hollow, fluted column of Portland stone, commemorates the Great Fire of 1666, which virtually destroyed London. Designed by Sir Christopher Wren (who deplored certain features added by others), it is 202 feet high, and the view from the caged gallery on top is well worth the admission price of sixpence and the effort of climbing the 311 steps inside. Here, all of old London lies below and around you, enabling you to see parts, at least, of literally dozens of famous buildings which have hitherto been only pictures and descriptions in books. Perhaps this experience will also enable you to decide which of these you would like to investigate further and which you would rather leave for another time.

Facing in the direction from which you have come, there is the Tower and the docks beyond, with the Thames snaking eastward to the distant sea. To the left, you glimpse a multitude of enterprises, large and small, proclaiming London's dominant role in national and international trade. Soaring up from among these temples of commerce are the lovely spires of many historic churches, including, most notably, those designed by Wren. There are thirty in all, of which thirteen have survived the ravages of time, builders, and the blitz, while the remainder still retain in their standing towers some vestige of their former glory. Space does not permit listing these noble buildings, but the interested visitor will find their names, locations, and dates, together with illuminating information and comment, in London Transport's booklet, "Christopher Wren."

To the north is the **Royal Exchange**, founded by Sir Thomas Gresham; from the steps leading up to its Corinthian portico royal proclamations are traditionally read. The **Bank of England**, to the left of this, has lost the considerable architectural interest it once had, as recent enlargement has obscured the work of Sir John Soane, its builder between 1788 and 1808. To the left of the Bank and beyond it is **Guildhall**, off Cheapside: the building dates from the 15th century, and its medieval walls escaped the bombs of 1940 as they had the flames of 1666. The scene of many a gorgeous banquet, Guildhall has been the seat of the City's government for over 500 years, as its site was for another 500 before that. **Mansion House**, standing between us and Guildhall at the Bank Crossing, has been the official residence of London's Lord Mayor since it was built by George Dance the elder, between 1739 and 1753.

Further to the left in the distance is the **General Post Office** and beyond, **St. Bartholomew's Hospital**. And finally we come to that vast upswelling dome of Wren's finest creation, St. Paul's.

ST. PAUL'S CATHEDRAL

As cathedral church of the diocese of London, St. Paul's has always been the favorite church of the city. While the present St. Paul's is, of course, junior by centuries to its great "rival" in Westminster, its known antecedents reach back considerably further into the past. Tradition has it that an early Christian church on the site was destroyed by backsliding Romans, who raised a temple to Diana in its stead. The first church of St. Paul's, Ludgate Hill, of which we have certain knowledge, was erected in the 7th century and destroyed by fire in 1087. Reconstruction was immediately begun, but the second St. Paul's was not finally finished until the 13th century. Both churches took their name, incidentally, from the legend according to which the apostle visited England at the time of Boadicea.

Old St. Paul's was one of the wonders of Europe—longer, wider and taller than the present structure, which is by far the biggest ecclesiastical building in England and second only to St. Peter's in all Christendom. The old nave, known as Paul's Walk, was used as a common thoroughfare and marketplace. In defiance of an Act of the

London roofs: looking from the Monument to St. Paul's

Common Council of London and a royal proclamation, it continued to be the scene of armed encounters and amorous escapades, and the general hiring place for servants (Shakespeare has Falstaff hire Bardolph there). In 1628, one Bishop Earle indignantly complained that "Paul's Walk is the land's epitome ... the noise is like that of bees ... a kind of still roar ... it is the general mint of all famous lies ... it is the thieves' sanctuary, who rob more safely in the crowd than a wilderness, whilst every searcher is a bush to hide them. It is the other expense of the day, after plays, taverns, and a bawdy-house; and men have still some oaths left to swear there." John Donne, the great metaphysical poet, was Dean of St. Paul's at the time.

Under the Commonwealth the enormous and ramshackle old edifice fell further into decay, and in 1666 young Christopher Wren had barely submitted his recommendations for its repair when London's glory was reduced to ashes. The fire burned for five full days.

Old St. Paul's, a medieval creation, had naturally been Gothic. Wren had studied in France and been inspired by the Renaissance ideas of Bramante, Palladio, and others, which had found expression throughout Latin Europe in monumental works of unprecedented simplicity and grandeur. He abominated the Gothic style, and if left to his own devices would unquestionably have built St. Paul's more nearly on the model of St. Peter's. His royal patron, Charles II, who had himself been reared in France, was generally sympathetic with Wren's aim but had many other pressing claims on his attention, affairs of the heart and state. Like sculptors Henry Moore and Sir Jacob Epstein in our own time, Wren had to contend with a large, powerful and entrenched body of profoundly conservative opinion, bent on seeing to it that the new structure was as much like the old as possible. Again and again his designs were rejected because they departed "too far from the Gothic." And when, at long last, he produced a plan which satisfied everyone, he took the precaution of obtaining the King's permission to make whatever modifications he might think desirable as construction proceeded. On numerous occasions during the forty-five years in which St. Paul's was a-building (1675–1710), Wren availed himself of this permission, and the cathedral of today differs in important respects from the original design.

62   London

Architecturally, St. Paul's represents a brilliant marriage between Gothic structure and Renaissance presentation. Cruciform in plan, its Gothic features—transepts, chancel, aisles, and even flying buttresses—are all skillfully clothed in the décor of early Baroque. Its interior is a triumph of cool and ordered near-perfection. Here can be seen the exquisite handiwork of Wren's talented assistants, among them Thornhill (frescoes in the dome), Tijou (wrought-iron screens), Cibber and Bird (various monuments and stone carvings) and Grinling Gibbons, the greatest of English woodcarvers, who fashioned the exceedingly beautiful choir stalls.

After about 1790 it became the custom to bury fallen military commanders of the Napoleonic Wars in St. Paul's, and the tradition has persisted. Most of the sculptured monuments of these warrior heroes are undistinguished. There are, however, two earlier memorials in the cathedral which should not be missed. The first is the inscription above Wren's simple tomb in the crypt; in this setting the famous words, *Lector, si monumentum requiris, circumspice* ("Reader, if you seek my monument, look around you"), take on their full significance. The second, on the south wall of the choir, is an effigy of Dr. Donne, the poet, standing wrapped in a shroud, like a ghost. This work, executed in 1631, started a grisly fad for upright shrouded effigies for tomb decoration. It was one of the very small number of objects in the old St. Paul's salvaged after the Great Fire.

Most visitors will want to climb to the **Whispering Gallery** in the dome, not only to test its celebrated property of making the slightest whisper audible around its circumference, but also to appreciate the size and admirable proportions of the central space beneath. From here, by stepping out onto the **Stone Gallery**, you can obtain a view of London, surpassed only by that from the **Golden Gallery**, higher up, which rings the base of the lantern above the dome. Still higher, in the little **Ball Room** above the lantern, you can look down onto the cathedral floor 300 feet below, and gain a lasting impression of the vast dimensions of St. Paul's.

On the day before Thanksgiving, 1958, the war-damaged East End of the cathedral was dedicated as the **American Chapel** in the presence of Queen Elizabeth and Vice President Nixon. This exquisite shrine in the City of London's most sacred hall contains a fine golden *baldacchino*, with twisting pillars, in keeping with Wren's original Baroque conception. Here, too, are, the arms of the American states in stained glass, wood carvings of American birds and wild animals, and a magnificently bound volume in which are inscribed the names of all the American soldiers, sailors and airmen based in Britain who gave their lives in the Second World War.

FROM ST. PAUL'S TO TRAFALGAR SQUARE

Descending Ludgate Hill from St. Paul's, you soon come to **Ludgate Circus**, where once hung a plaque honoring John Wilkes, the ir-

64 London

Somerset House was named after the Protector, the Duke of Somerset, who was building a great palace on the site when he was executed in 1552. In like manner, the names of several streets leading off the Strand recall the noblemen of Stuart times, whose mansions and gardens extended down to the river. In this category are Bedford, Villiers and Southampton Streets. Until the 1920s, there was an amusing street sequence along the south side of the Strand which ran as follows: *George* Street, *Villiers* Street, *Duke* Street, *Of* Alley, *Buckingham* Street. Just south of the Strand is the Queen's **Chapel of the Savoy** (Savoy Chapel). This is the private property of all British monarchs, who are, irrespective of sex, Dukes of Lancaster. When the national anthem is sung there, it begins, "God save our gracious Queen, Long live our noble Duke...." Two short blocks north of the Strand is old **Covent Garden** with its church of **St. Paul's**, "the handsomest barn in England." Built by Inigo Jones in 1638 and restored in 1795, St. Paul's has been closely linked with the theatre throughout its history. Lewis Hallam, an associate of the tempestuous actor Charles Macklin, who is buried there, went to America in 1752 and spent many years in the colonies with his troupe, the American Company; this was our permanent repertory group, and Hallam has often been called the father of the American theatre. The east face of St. Paul's, fronting on old Covent Garden, was the place where Eliza Doolittle had the encounter with Professor Higgins that led to "Pygmalion" and "My Fair Lady." A number of earlier "musicals"—the operettas of Messrs. Gilbert and Sullivan—had their premieres nearby, at the Savoy Theatre on the Strand.

The Strand ends at Trafalgar Square, which is dominated by an 18-foot statue of Lord Nelson standing on a column of Devon granite nearly 185 feet high. The Square is a favorite place for political demonstrations and is infested with cacaphonous starlings, but is notable in this brief survey for three structures: the **Admiralty Arch**, the church of **St. Martin's-in-the-Fields**, and the **National Gallery**. This first is a massive archway spanning the entrance to the Mall, which leads straight to Buckingham Palace and is the route of most state processions. The second, often called the "Admiralty Church," was built by James Gibbs, a pupil of Wren's, in 1726. The third, rudely dubbed the "National Cruet Stand" when it went up in 1838, is of small architectural interest; however, it houses one of the world's finest collections of paintings of all schools. The **National Portrait Gallery** behind it contains the likenesses of the "greats" of English history. While these paintings were chosen more for the fame of their subjects than for their artistic merits, several artists of stature are represented, including Holbein, Van Dyck, Lely, Kneller, Hogarth, Romney, Gainsborough, Reynolds, and our own John Singer Sargent. In front of the National Gallery stand statues of two men who would hardly have been accorded such an honor in their own day: James II, who had to flee the country in 1688—and

The Bank of England; St. Martin's Tower

George Washington. The portico of the building affords a fine view down Whitehall.

FROM TRAFALGAR SQUARE TO WESTMINSTER ABBEY

Whitehall, which extends only to Richmond Terrace, where it becomes Parliament Street, takes its name from the old Whitehall Palace, Henry VIII's favorite town residence. Of this rambling structure the part that remains is happily its best—the **Banqueting House**, begun by Inigo Jones in 1619. As noted in the previous chapter, contemporary Whitehall is a famous street of government buildings, but it is rich in historical associations as well. From its Trafalgar Square end, King Charles I, on horseback, looks down it to the place where he was beheaded, on a platform at the corner of the Banqueting House that is now the United Services Museum (containing relics of Britain's fighting services and dioramas showing fifteen great battles). A foundryman, John Rivett, is said to have secretly buried it when it was sold to him by the Roundheads with the command that he destroy it, exhibiting a heap of broken metal to prove that he had complied, and then, having for years reaped a tidy sum from the sale of souvenir scraps to mourning Cavaliers and triumphant Roundheads, to have dug the statue up again, following the Restoration, and presented it with due ceremony to the subject's royal son.

Descending Whitehall, you find, on your right, the **Admiralty**, the **Horse Guards**, the **Treasury**, the **Home Office**, and the **Ministry of Defence** (British spelling). On the left are the **Ministry of Agriculture**, the **War Office**, and the **Office of the Lord Privy Seal**. Of this collection the building called Horse Guards deserves special mention. This is a beautifully proportioned edifice designed by William Kent in 1753; before it a mounted guard is still posted—changed daily at 11 A.M. and inspected at 4 P.M. in ceremonies which attract numerous visitors, British and foreign. **Horse Guards Parade**, behind the building through the central archway, is the site of the annual ritual of "Trooping the Colour" in honor of the sovereign's birthday: a gorgeous spectacle in scarlet, blue, silver, and gold against the green of St. James's Park and the mellow gray Portland stone of Horse Guards.

Just before you reach the **Cenotaph**, Britain's simple and impressive memorial to her sons who fell in two World Wars, you come to one of the most famous thoroughfares in the world, **Downing Street**. Strange to relate, the builder who bequeathed his name to the street on which the British Prime Minister has his home at no. 10 was a Harvard man. Sir George Downing lived in Massachusetts from 1638 to 1645. It is unlikely, however, that his great alma mater takes much pride in this particular son, who was thoroughly detested by Pepys, and whose character, according to the *Encyclopedia Britannica*, was "marked by treachery, servility, and ingratitude."

At the foot of Parliament Street you emerge onto Parliament Square. On your left the great **Clock Tower** looms up to the huge round face of Big Ben (actually the name of the 13-ton bell, but familiarly used for the clock) and higher still to its fantastic 316-foot pinnacle. Right of it are the **Houses of Parliament** and ancient **Westminster Hall**, with the 336-foot **Victoria Tower** rising behind them. Directly across from you is Tudor **St. Margaret's Church**, and beyond it, partly screened by trees, the huge irregular shape of **Westminster Abbey**. Ringing the central lawn in the foreground are statues of great statesmen; the one farthest to the right shows Abraham Lincoln standing, deep in thought, before a Grecian chair. This figure, the only one here of a man who owed no allegiance to the British Crown, is a full-sized replica of the famous work by Augustus St. Gaudens, in Chicago.

This surprisingly small plot of ground, with Westminster Abbey on one side and the Houses of Parliament on another, is the very heart of the British Commonwealth of Nations and the focal point of Britain's history since the Conquest.

The Houses of Parliament, with their two great square towers and slender Gothic **Central Tower**, comprise a single building, erected after a disastrous fire in 1834. Together with medieval Westminster Hall, St. Stephen's Hall and Porch, and certain modern offices, they

Houses of Parliament and Westminster Bridge

Historic London 67

make up what is properly called the **Palace of Westminster**. Space does not permit a detailed description of this vast conglomeration, but we can, at least, identify its most important parts before moving on to our destination.

When Parliament is in session, a Union Jack flies from the Victoria Tower by day and a light shines in the Clock Tower by night. At such times Westminster Hall is open to the public from 10 A.M. to 1:30 P.M. Monday to Thursday, and from 10 A.M. to 5 P.M. Saturday. During a parliamentary recess, it is open every weekday from 10 A.M. to 4 P.M. To enter this ancient hall is to return to the time when the White Tower was a-building; it was erected between 1097 and 1099 by William Rufus. Only the side walls of the original structure remain, but the dimensions are unchanged. In its day, Westminster Hall was probably the biggest single building in the known world that was neither a church nor a fortress. When a banquet guest expressed his astonishment at its enormous size, his arrogant host, the King, casually replied that, "It is but a bed-chamber to the palace that I will ere long raise up." The following year, however, William lay lifeless under a tree in the New Forest, the victim of an arrow from an unknown hand.

In 1394, King Richard II caused the by-then-dilapidated pile to be rebuilt, adding, in particular, a vast and intricately carved roof of oak from Sussex trees planted in the sixth century. This roof not only was, but still is a world wonder. One of the finest feats of carpentry extant, it makes Westminster Hall, in the judgment of the normally reserved Royal Commission, "probably the finest timber-roofed building in Europe." When, in this century, replacements were needed for some of the original timbers, owing to the ravages of death-watch beetles, they were supplied by a Member of Parliament who was a direct descendant of the original supplier, from trees that were over 600 years old and hence had been standing when the roof was first constructed.

Historically, Westminster Hall is, with the Tower of London, one of the two most important secular buildings in Britain. Every important state trial from the time of Rufus until the last century took place within it. There, Guy Fawkes was condemned to be hanged, drawn and quartered for his part in the Gunpowder Plot; there Charles I received his death sentence, and Oliver Cromwell had himself formally declared Lord Protector of England, borrowing the Coronation Chair from Westminster Abbey for the purpose. And there, after a seven-year trial in which he was furiously denounced by Burke, Fox, and Sheridan, Warren Hastings was finally acquitted of all charges arising out of his conduct as the first Governor-General of India.

The Houses of Parliament can be seen by tour on Saturdays, Bank Holidays, Mondays, Tuesdays, and Thursdays in August, and Thursdays in September from 10:00 to 5:00. To see the Commons or Lords in session takes time—you can probably get into the public gallery by joining the line (that is, the queue) at the St. Stephen's Hall entrance. The public is admitted after 2:30 Monday to Thursday and after 11:00 A.M. Friday. If you know a Member or have English friends who do, he or she may be able to provide you with a ticket entitling you to earlier admission. Tickets can sometimes be obtained through the American Embassy in Grosvenor Square (499-9000).

Dwarfed by its giant neighbors, little **St. Margaret's**, since 1614 the official church of the House of Commons, is too often overlooked by visitors. This is particularly regrettable in view of the fact that this lovely Tudor building, which dates from 1523, has a number of American associations. Raleigh, the founder of Virginia, was buried there after his execution in the Old Palace Yard; he is commemorated by a tablet and by the West Window, the gift of American citizens, with some lines by James Russell Lowell, our Minister in London at the time of the presentation. A mosaic commemorates Bishop Phillips Brooks of Massachusetts, who often preached there. Our Ambassador reads the Lessons there at an annual service on Memorial Day.

The glory of St. Margaret's, however, is the *East Window,* probably the most beautiful example of stained glass in England. It was a gift to Henry VII from Columbus' patrons, Ferdinand and Isabella of Spain, on the betrothal of their daughter Catharine of Aragon to Henry's son Arthur. By the time it was delivered from Flanders, however, Catharine was married to Henry VIII, and the latter, taking no special pleasure in the sight of his bride with his deceased brother, packed it off to Waltham Abbey. It found its way to St. Margaret's in 1758.

The church contains many interesting monuments, including one to an influential Elizabethan courtier who "died a meide in the eighte two years of her age the twelfe of Februaryte 1589." William Caxton, the first English printer, is buried in the churchyard.

WESTMINSTER ABBEY

It is impossible to overemphasize the importance of this unique national shrine both in English history and in the affections of the British people, to whom it is simply "The Abbey." It was founded by Edward the Confessor. Legend has it that a Roman temple to Apollo stood on what was then the marshy Thames island of Thorney, a companion to Diana's temple in Londinium. Another legend, carefully nurtured by the Abbey's medieval monks, tells how a 7th-century church there was consecrated by St. Peter in person. Arriving on the Lambeth side of the river, he got a fisherman to ferry him over; no sooner had he entered the newly erected church than it "suddenly seemed on fire with a glow that enkindled the firmament." Simultaneously, a choir of angels burst into song, and the church walls were sprinkled with holy oil and water. Then St. Peter emerged, he in-

Memorial to Ben Jonson in the Abbey

structed the awe-stricken fisherman to report to the bishop that his church had been properly sanctified, and added: "For yourself, go out into the river; you will catch a plentiful supply of fish, whereof the larger part shall be salmon." For centuries the Thames fishermen contributed a tenth of their earnings to the Abbey, whose official title is the Collegiate Church of St. Peter in Westminster. A series of tiles in the Chapter House illustrates the story.

In 1066 the Confessor's remains were laid to rest in the new Abbey, and that Christmas Day William the Conqueror had himself crowned there. Thus were established, within a short span of months, two precedents which were to have far-reaching consequences. For 700 years, nearly all English monarchs were interred in the Abbey, George II (died 1760) being the last; and from William I to Elizabeth II the coronation of all but two kings and queens of England have taken place within its hallowed walls. With the Reformation, monarchs became officially Head of the Church of England, and the Abbey, as "holy of the holies," has remained a "royal peculiar," exempt from the authority of bishop or archbishop, since the time of the first Elizabeth.

The present building dates principally from the reign of Henry III (13th century) with numerous later additions which include, most notably as far as the exterior is concerned, the twin towers at the western entrance, designed by Wren and completed by his pupil Hawksmoor in 1740. Henry VII's exquisite chapel at the other end, opposite the Houses of Parliament, is pure Tudor Gothic. It would be impractical to continue this discussion further, for the complicated architectural history of the 900-year-old Abbey and its precincts would fill a volume. The story does, indeed, form the subject of not one but several excellent books, which are readily obtainable and sure to be of consuming interest to students of English architecture.

A person who wants to get the most out of his visit to the Abbey should devote at least an hour to perambulating its walks, inspecting the monuments which strike his fancy and reading the inscriptions thereon—touching, philosophical, poetic, whimsical, and tinged, occasionally, with unconscious humor. The custom of interring notable

Westminster Abbey, where Britain's monarchs are crowned

sons and daughters of England in the Abbey began so long ago that it would be impossible to list even its tombs here, let alone the hundreds of statues, busts, plaques and other memorials it contains. A guide to the Abbey's tombs appeared as early as 1600. These are of an almost incredible variety—as are the individuals they memorialize. They include, together with kings and queens, such humble subjects as Philip Clark, "plumber to this collegiate church," and Elizabeth Atkinson, "body laundress to Queen Anne"; John Broughton, a prize fighter, and Ann Oldfield, an actress; and Thomas Parr, an ancient Shropshire farmhand whose only claim to fame—and claim it certainly was—was that he had reached the ripe old age of 152 when he died in 1635.

Entering the Abbey by the great west doors between the towers, you find yourself at the **Tomb of the Unknown Warrior**, commemorating the one million British dead of Word War I. From here, the glory of the loftiest nave in England can be appreciated to the full. Straight ahead is the high altar and reredos, and behind it the **Chapel of Edward the Confessor**, king and saint, whose shrine is still the center of his church even though it was despoiled by Henry VIII and later by the Puritans. Close at hand stands the **Coronation Chair**, made in 1300, containing the Stone of Scone, back in place again after being stolen on Christmas morning, 1950, and transported north to its original homeland by a band of ardent young Scottish Nationalists. Radiating out from the Confessor's tomb are lovely chapels. The most splendid of these is that of Henry VII, with its marvelous fan-

Historic London

tracery roof and its truly gorgeous display of banners of the Knights of the Bath. Here are buried no fewer than five kings and five queens. Originally, Henry VII intended to make this chapel a shrine for his father, for whose canonization he applied to the Pope; on learning the price, however, he changed his mind and ordained it for his own glorification instead.

On the north side of the nave is the inscription, "O rare Ben Johnson" (*sic*), where the poet was buried standing up, in accordance with his instructions.

In front of the choir screen, on the south side, are the graves of Isaac Newton, Lord Kelvin and Charles Darwin. In the **Musicians' Corner** nearby are the graves of Henry Purcell and John Blow. **Statesmen's Corner** has monuments to Pitt and Fox, Peel and Palmerston, Disraeli and Gladstone. But the most visited spot in Westminster Abbey is the so-called **Poets' Corner**. Here are the graves of Chaucer, Spenser, Dryden, Johnson, Tennyson, Browning, Dickens, Hardy, and Kipling, and memorials to Shakespeare (with lines from "The Tempest" wrongly quoted), Milton, Burns, Coleridge, Southey, Wordsworth, and Ruskin. Here, too, is a bust of Henry Wadsworth Longfellow, placed there by English admirers in the last century.

American colonial days are recalled in several monuments. Among these is one to General Wolfe, the victor of Quebec in the French and Indian War; he is shown stark naked, but supported by an officer in full regimentals. In another piece, British troops who fought at Ticonderoga in the same struggle are depicted dressed as Romans. There is also in the Abbey a remarkable monument to Major André, the young British officer who was executed as a spy during the Revolution.

No visitor, if he can possibly avoid it, should miss the **museum** in the crypt. The undercroft, the last surviving fragment of the Confessor's Abbey, is beautiful in itself. And the waxen effigies of kings, queens and great personages, which were formerly made to be displayed at their subjects' funeral processions, are wondrously lifelike. Particularly interesting are the figures of Charles II, and of Arabella, *La Belle Stuart,* who eloped with the Duke of Richmond to escape Charles' amorous attentions.

The superb octagonal **Chapter House** in which Parliament met for 170 years should also be seen; and a stroll through the **Cloisters**, still impregnated with the timeless peace that is the legacy of the Benedictine monks who lived here for so many centuries, is an ideal way to end your visit to the church of the British people.

OTHER HISTORIC POINTS IN CENTRAL LONDON

In the City, among the historic churches that were *not* built by Wren, four are especially worthy of attention. **All Hallows, Barking-by-the-Tower** is one of great antiquity. It has a Saxon doorway and cross, and, in the crypt, abundant Roman remains including tessellated pavements. The tower is the only example of Cromwellian church building in the City, as All Hallows escaped the Great Fire. Here, William Penn was baptized in 1644, and John Quincy Adams married.

In the Bishopsgate quarter, **St. Helen's** is notable for its curious relics from Tudor, Elizabethan and Stuart times; and humble **St. Ethelburga's** for its medieval front and for three stained-glass windows (modern) dedicated to the adventures of Henry Hudson. Fortunately for us, the flames stopped short of Bishopsgate in 1666.

St. Bartholomew-the-Great, near Smithfield Market, is the oldest and most interesting church in London. It is all that remains of the Priory of St. Bartholomew founded in 1123 by the monk Rahere, who also founded the hospital of the same name, London's first, across the way. It is an altogether magnificent example of apsidal Norman architecture, and its fascinating relics include the tomb and effigy of its founder.

The house at **17 Gough Square**, E. C. 4, in which Dr. Johnson lived while he was compiling his great *Dictionary* is a good example of Queen Anne domestic architecture. The **College of Arms**, in Queen Victoria Street, dates from 1683; its genealogical and heraldic library is the finest in the world.

Historic places in Southwark, across the river, include **Southwark Cathedral**, which has Norman remains and a perfect early English Lady Chapel. Off Borough High Street is the **George Inn**, dating from 1677, the last galleried hostel left in London. It is possible that Shakespeare knew the earlier George and certain that Dickens knew this one. In Lambeth, to the west, are **Lambeth Palace** (previously noted) and adjacent **St. Mary's Church**, with a 15th-century tower and some interesting tombs, including that of Captain (later Admiral) Bligh, of *Bounty* fame.

Across the river, in Westminster, tucked away behind the Abbey, is a massive stone building known as the **Jewel Tower**. Built in 1365, it is, together with Westminster Hall, virtually all that remains above ground of the old Palace of Westminster. **Westminster School**, in the Dean's Yard, was mentioned in 1339 but refounded by Queen Elizabeth in 1560. It is one of the oldest and best of England's famous "public" schools. A playful ritual called "Tossing the Pancake" is enacted here annually on Shrove Tuesday. A large pancake is tossed over "the bar," and in the scramble that ensues the boy who retrieves the largest piece of it is awarded £1.05. He often gets his picture in the papers, too.

The **Roman Catholic Westminster Cathedral**, near Victoria Station, is the seat of England's only Cardinal. It was completed in 1903. The gallery of its 284-foot tower (with elevator service) commands a fine view of London. Eric Gill, whose influence on British art was paramount in his day, fashioned the bas-reliefs that are the Stations of the Cross.

Cleopatra's Needle in the Embankment Gardens

By far the oldest object in London, though certainly not very English, is the Egyptian obelisk miscalled **Cleopatra's Needle**, near Charing Cross on the Victoria Embankment. It is one of a pair erected at Heliopolis about 1500 B.C., and its twin is in Central Park, New York. Of the historic vessels permanently moored to Victoria Embankment, the only one which the public is allowed to board is **H.M.S. Discovery**, which Captain Scott took to Antarctica in 1901, the year of her launching. Scott's cabin is shown, together with relics including letters and personal belongings.

From Trafalgar Square, passing under the Admiralty Arch into the broad avenue known as the Mall that leads to Buckingham Palace between Green Park and St. James's Park, you enter the quarter of St. James's. The first thing you encounter is a very tall column surmounted by a statue of George III's second son. This particular Duke of York was distinguished for nothing whatever, unless it was the fact that he was perpetually in financial difficulties; when his handsome statue was erected in 1833, some said he had been placed so high to avoid his creditors, and others conjectured that the lightning rod on his head was a spike for his bills. **Marlborough House**, farther on, was designed by Wren for Sir Winston Churchill's great military ancestor, the first Duke of Marlborough. **St. James's Palace**, beyond it, was built by Henry VIII. Until Queen Victoria took up residence in Buckingham Palace, it was the London home of successive sovereigns, which explains why ambassadors to Britain are accredited "to the Court of St. James's." The *gatehouse,* at the foot of St. James's Street, off Piccadilly, is a fine example of Tudor brickwork. There are two noteworthy chapels attached to the palace—that of the original building (1552) with a magnificent ceiling attributed to Holbein,

Lincoln's Inn, one of the inns of court

and another, in Marlborough Gate, known as the **Queen's Chapel**, because it was designed by Inigo Jones, Wren's great forerunner, for Charles I's queen, Henrietta Maria. This chapel, with its Carolean paneling, its royal pews and its ornate roof, is a little architectural masterpiece too little known.

Buckingham Palace, (where St. James's, Westminster and Belgravia meet) is, of course, the permanent London residence of Queen Elizabeth and the Duke of Edinburgh. When the Queen is there, the royal standard flies at the masthead, day and night. The palace was originally built for the Duke of Buckingham in 1703, but has been altered many times since, notably in 1913 when the front was entirely refaced.

St. James's Church, Piccadilly, is the only West End church designed by Wren (1684). It contains a font and an altarpiece by Grinling Gibbons. Mayfair's most remarkable church is **St. George's**, Hanover Square. Built between 1713 and 1724 by John James, yet another of Wren's numerous pupils, it has been famous since the early 19th century for its fashionable weddings. Shelley, Disraeli and Theodore Roosevelt were all married there.

Moving southwest to Chelsea you find **Chelsea Hospital**, founded by Charles II in 1682, some say at the instigation of his mistress, Nell Gwyn. The buildings were begun by Wren, added to by Robert Adam, and completed by Sir John Soane. The statue of the hospital's founder is by Grinling Gibbons, and the lovely gardens which extend to the Embankment are the setting of the world-famous Chelsea Flower Show in late May.

Historic London 75

Westward along the river is **Thomas Carlyle's house** (24 Cheyne Row, S. W. 3), where the writer lived for nearly fifty years. It has been left as he knew it, as a memorial museum to him. A few paces farther on is **Chelsea Old Church** now fully restored after being almost destroyed by a bomb; this was the church of Sir Thomas More, whose chapel, dating from 1528, happily survived the bombing intact. **Crosby Hall**, a few paces past the church, was the great hall of the 15th-century mansion of John Crosby, a wool merchant. It was moved here in 1910 from Bishopsgate to preserve it from demolition.

Fulham, to the west of Chelsea, is notable for **Fulham Palace**, the official residence of the Bishop of London, and for **All Saints' Church**, by Putney Bridge, whose tower dates from 1440 and whose interior is rich in monuments and brasses.

Kensington, to the north, is renowned for many things, but, in terms of history, principally for three: the **Albert Memorial, Kensington Palace**, and **Holland House**. The first, in Kensington Gardens opposite the Albert Hall, is surely one of the most ambitious and hideous monuments ever erected anywhere to anyone. It is also utterly captivating. The second, as noted earlier, was acquired by William of Orange as a royal residence. Wren designed its exterior and its remarkable Orangery. The palace now houses the **London Museum**. Lovely Holland Park marks the site of Holland House, destroyed in World War II; built in 1607, it was a regular meeting place for Whig writers and politicians during the late 18th and early 19th centuries. It is now the site of the central London Youth Hostel.

Tyburn, at the corner of Hyde Park that is now called Marble Arch, where the boroughs of Paddington, St. Marylebone, and Westminster come together, was for over 600 years London's foremost spot for public executions, a highly popular form of entertainment. The first known was in 1196 and the last in 1783. A wall tablet there recounts the grim story in outline.

In Bloomsbury, at **48 Doughty Street**, W. C. 1, is the house in which Charles Dickens wrote parts of the "Pickwick Papers," "Oliver Twist," "Nicholas Nickleby" and "Barnaby Rudge." Here is a Dickens library and manuscripts, and the writer's study as it was.

Holborn is the home of **Gray's Inn** and **Lincoln's Inn**. These lovely old Inns of Court should both be seen, as should Staple Inn, whose picturesque Tudor house-fronts, erected in 1586, look out on the street called Holborn. Dr. Johnson lived at Staple Inn for several months, and is said to have written "Rasselas" there in a single week to pay for his mother's funeral.

John Wesley's Chapel and House are at 47 City Road, E. C. 1, in Finsbury, adjoining Holborn on the east. The simple tomb of the founder of Methodism is in the center of the churchyard behind the Chapel. The house is a **Wesley Museum**, and a place of devoted pilgrimage for Methodists from all over the world.

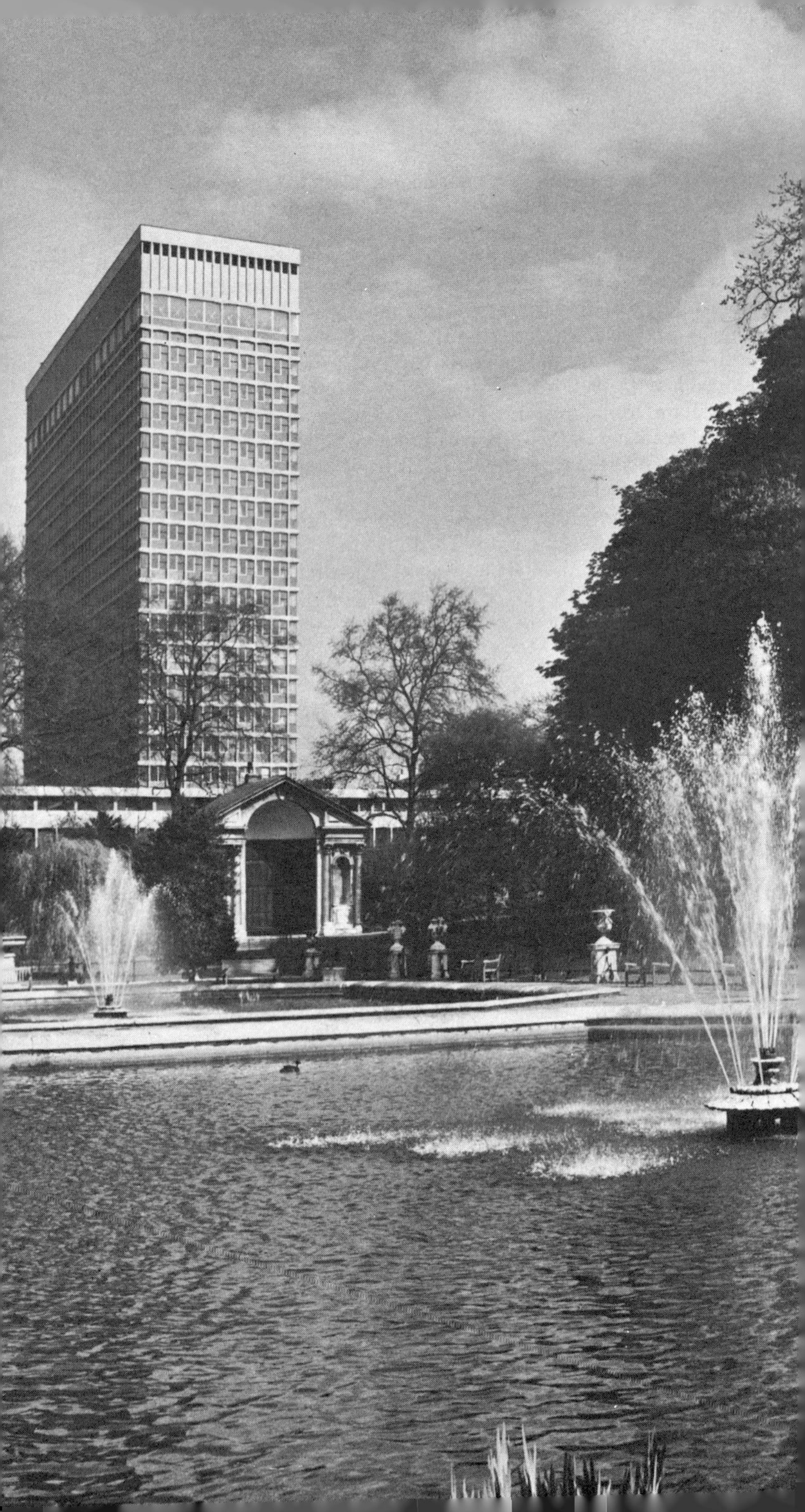

CHAPTER 6

WHERE TO STAY

As everywhere, prices in London have increased.

The past few years have seen the sprouting of many super-modern hotels, with many more on the drawing boards. The more "charming" older lodgings have in most cases been recently refurbished, and, in the case of the "irreproachables," the great grand standards have been maintained.

There are thousands of hotels in the city. To give anything like a complete account of all the accommodations available in a place the size of London would require a small book. This chapter is intended to give you as complete a picture as possible, over a broad price range, of the best accommodations available. By and large, the greatest number listed here are situated in the heart of the shopping and entertainment "downtown" areas of London, but also included are a good many quieter hotels out of the mainstream.

April through October are the busiest tourist months in England, as they are throughout most of the Continent, and despite the great number of rooms available in London, you will be wise to reserve early if you are to be sure of getting the kind of accommodations you want. The British Tourist Authority—which has offices at 680 Fifth Avenue in New York, 875 N. Michigan Avenue in Chicago, 1712 Commerce Street in Dallas, and 612 So. Flower Street in Los Angeles—can help you choose a hotel to fit your budget and preferences. Although the BTA cannot actually make the booking for you (that is the job of your airline or travel agent), it does provide very up-to-date hotel and restaurant data as well as any

The Royal Lancaster, one of London's new luxury hotels

78 London

other information that could possibly help the tourist. As it is a government organization whose function is to aid the tourist coming from abroad, all advice is reliable and brochures are gladly given, gratis. The BTA publishes a booklet entitled *Hotels and Restaurants in London* (15 p.) which any visitor will find immensely helpful. In London the BTA address is 64 St. James's Street S.W. 1 (tel. 629-9191).

London Hotels in General. It is perhaps not too far-fetched to say that London's hotels, considered *en masse,* brilliantly illustrate the opposition, so frequently encountered in other spheres, of two dominant English traits: a Cavalier love of pomp and a Puritan preference for austerity. The leading establishments are so steeped in romantic legend that one scarcely thinks of them as hotels; their names immediately conjure up visions of vast and sumptuous halls, richly carpeted and hung with priceless paintings, where enormous mirrors reflect a glamorous clientele, arrayed beneath crystal chandeliers, of turbaned maharajahs, tiara-ed duchesses, magnates, movie queens, and mysterious men in dark glasses plotting the downfall of Ruritanian dynasties. In a diehard minority of the smaller places, on the other hand, the virtues of simplicity are so firmly stressed that it becomes difficult to avoid the conclusion that as far as the management is concerned, conveniences like central heating and private plumbing are nothing but pernicious innovations which encourage slothfulness and sin. Needless to say, the great bulk of London hotels belong in neither of these categories, and none of the latter type is mentioned below.

Nevertheless it is just as well to realize that certain amenities which are standard in American hotels are not provided in London. For the very good reason that summers there are seldom uncomfortably hot, to cite one example, it is most unlikely that you will find an icewater tap in your bathroom. And air conditioning is, by and large, the exception rather than the rule. Even in some of the better hotels, the ratio of bathrooms to rooms often runs to no better than two to three. Most, however, do have professional services, such as hairdressers. These small inconveniences apart, you will be lucky indeed to encounter anywhere else the same high quality of efficient personal service that will be yours in the better London hotels.

Charges and Tips. On the all-important matter of costs there are two cautionary notes to be sounded. First, while the prices quoted below

Where to Stay

were the latest obtainable at the time this chapter was written, they are all subject to variation, and it is wise to confirm them before booking a room. Second, a number of London hotels have adopted the Continental practice of adding a surcharge to their bills—usually 12½ per cent of the total—in lieu of a tip. The symbol (S) has been inserted after the price range on the listings of hotels which make this charge. Value Added Tax (VAT) of 8% is included unless noted otherwise.

As for the vexing problem of how much to give the porter who carries your luggage or the bellboy who goes on errands for you, that will depend, of course, partly on the services rendered and partly on the nature of the hotel. When you have become familiar with British currency—a process which many Americans find trying by reason of the bewildering number and variety of the coins in use—this should become much less troublesome. A rough rule of thumb is to tip as you would in an equivalent American hotel, substituting ten new pence for a quarter. Remember that at most places, in accordance with European custom, you need not tip at all until you leave. Remember, too, that the manager and his staff are quite accustomed to giving advice on this subject, so that you need feel no embarrassment in asking them.

The "Top Twelve." London's fabled and truly first-rate hotels are all located in the city's stylish center: the West End, Westminster, and Mayfair. Most are to be found in this last district, the most fashionable of all, in the rectangular area bounded by Oxford and Bond Streets, Park Lane and Piccadilly. Each is stamped with its unique character, so that if you were to ask seasoned travelers to name the ten best hotels, they would have to name eleven, and their responses would faithfully mirror their own individual habits and idiosyncracies. Certain establishments, however, would be sure to figure on everybody's list: Claridge's, the Dorchester, and the Savoy. Others whose presence could be predicted with almost equal confidence are the Connaught, Grosvenor House, the Hyde Park, and the Ritz. If one of your travelers was the type who liked to surround himself with the atmosphere of the country he was visiting, he would probably name the Savoy. Conversely, a man who preferred the conveniences of the American hotel would undoubtedly include the Westbury, the Hilton, the Londonderry and the Inn on the Park.

Grosvenor House is one of London's finest

80 London

You must book well in advance to be sure of being granted admission to these hallowed halls. Brief notes on the hotels named follow.

Dollar equivalents are computed at $2.00 to the pound, the rate in effect at this printing. Be sure to recheck the rate of exchange before you make your reservation.

The Berkeley, Wilton Place, S.W.1. 235-6000 (150 rooms, all with baths). A new and elegantly decorated hotel on a residential street in Knightsbridge. Interior includes chandeliers, panelling and French furniture; other features are a swimming pool, a sauna and a cinema. Its "Perroquet Restaurant" is fashionable for lunch. *Singles from £20.00 ($40), doubles from £28.00 ($56.00).*

Claridge's, Brook Street, W.1, 629-8860 (265 bedrooms, all with baths). A short walk from "Little America" (Grosvenor Square) and just about the ultimate in dignified swank. With no fewer than 55 private sitting rooms, it is also the ultimate in privacy. It is the favorite haunt of visiting royalty. Garage. *Singles from £18.00 ($36.00), doubles from £28.00 ($54.00) plus 15% S.*

The Connaught, Carlos Place, W.1, 499-7070 (109 bedrooms, all with baths). A splendid late-Victorian building between Berkeley and Grosvenor Squares, with a reassuringly sombre interior of darkly gleaming woodwork and polished brass. Friendly in a discreet British way, with a loyal following. *Singles from £17.00 ($34.00), doubles from £25.00 ($50.00). (S. 15%)*

The Dorchester, Park Lane, W.1, 629-8888 (278 rooms, all with baths). Flamboyant 1930's architecture with a comfortable and stylish interior. In Hyde Park. Sought after by celebrities and businessmen seeking a good address and efficient telephone service. Garage. *Singles from £17.50 ($35.00), doubles from £29.00 ($58.00).*

Grosvenor House, Park Lane, W.1, 499-6363 (478 rooms, all with baths). Just up Park Lane from the Dorchester, this palatial hotel much resembles its neighbor and caters to much the same clientele—although, for no apparent reason, it is ever so slightly behind it in cachet. Excellent food, drinks, and service. Swimming pool, sauna and garage. *Singles from £20.00 ($40.00), doubles from £28.00 ($54.00). (S. 12½%)*

The Hilton, Park Lane, W.1, 493-8000 (510 rooms, all with baths). New, and a skyscraper by London standards. Luxurious, a reminder of America but with views of Hyde Park and Buckingham Palace. *Singles from £19.00 ($38.00), doubles from £24.00 ($48.00). (S. 12½%)*

The Hyde Park, Knightsbridge, S.W.1, 235-2000 (168 rooms, all with baths. Just redone). A spacious and imposing relic from the good old days before World War I, located (like New York's Plaza, which it vaguely resembles) close to some of the country's finest shops. It commands a magnificent view of Hyde Park and is much favored by country families in town for the season. *Singles from £19.00 ($38.00), doubles from £22.00 ($44.00). (S. 12½%)*

Inn on the Park, Hamilton Place, Park Lane, W.1, 499-0888 (228 rooms, all with baths). A luxury hotel overlooking Hyde Park, completed in 1969. All modern hotel facilities are available. *Singles from £19 ($38.00), doubles from £25.00 ($50.00). (S. 12½%)*

Where to Stay

The Londonderry, Park Lane, W. 1, 493-7292 (150 rooms, all with baths). A new luxury hotel built near the Hilton on the site of the former home of the Marquess of Londonderry. *Singles from £17.00 ($34.00), doubles from £20.00 ($40.00).*

The Ritz, Piccadilly, W. 1, 493-8181 (120 rooms, all with baths). All that need be said is that this establishment lives up to its name. Outside, its arcaded entrance and mansard upper story give it a Parisian look, particularly appropriate for a great international hotel in the Continental tradition. *Singles from £17.00 ($34.00), doubles from £27.00 ($54.00). Suites £40 ($80.00). (S. 10½%)*

The Savoy, Victoria Embankment, W.C. 2, 836-4343 (319 rooms, all with baths). Facing the Thames on one side, it is just off the Strand, London's "Rialto," on the other. Like its younger rival, the Dorchester, it is much patronized by headliners, as it has been ever since it was built by the fabulous impresario D'Oyly Carte. Garage. *Singles from £17.50 ($35.00), doubles from £25.00 ($50.00). (S. 15%)*

The Westbury, New Bond Street, W. 1, 629-7755 (279 rooms, all with baths). At this London link in the Knott chain the key word is "American"; the hotel even flies the Stars and Stripes from its rooftop. The cuisine is chiefly Yankee (and Rebel), as are the plumbing, the decor, and the color T.V. set in every suite. Immediate access to some of the world's smartest shops. Garage. *Singles from £14.00 ($28.00), doubles from £18.00 ($36.00). (S. 12½%)*

Other Good Hotels in the Center. There are so many more good hotels in London's fashionable center (including several which would rank in the "top twelve" on some people's lists) that it is difficult to make a choice. The selection offered below was made after careful checking of some twenty-five recommended hotels, against such criteria as price, location, facilities provided, percentage of rooms with private baths, and size of the rooms, together with certain less easily defined factors like friendliness and charm. It is, of course, perfectly possible that you may find another hotel in the area, omitted here, which may suit you even better.

The prices quoted after each hotel listed are those charged for the cheapest single room and the most expensive double room; with the exception of hotels which provide bathrooms with every room the first figure will therefore be that of a single room *without* bath. All prices here (unlike the "top twelve") include breakfast except where

The Savoy is almost as much a part of London lore as Buckingham Palace.

London

BNI (breakfast not included) follows the listing. *S* indicates service charge added to base price. Prices are given in *pounds* only, since the rate of exchange tends to fluctuate. But the chart is included to give you some idea of how your hotel bill will translate into dollars:

£	$	£	$
.50	1.00	2	4.00
1.00	2.00	5	10.00
1.25	2.50	10	20.00
1.50	3.00	15	30.00
1.75	3.50	20	40.00

The Athenaeum, 116 Piccadilly, W. 1 499-3464 (115 rooms, all with baths). Rebuilt and remodeled. Overlooking Green Park. *£17 to £25. S. BNI.*

Brown's, Dover Street, W. 1, 493-6020 (137 rooms with baths). Loaded with atmosphere of the Edwardian variety, and a favorite of Americans. *£15.50 to £28.*

Capitol, Basil Street, S.W. 3 589-5171 (60 rooms with baths). New and smallish. Superb cuisine. *£17 to £24. S. 15%.*

Carlton Tower, Cadogan Place, S.W. 1, 235-5411 (323 rooms and suites, all with baths). Tower hotel, new, deluxe. Fine restaurants. Garage. *£12 to £21.50. S. 15%.*

The Cumberland, Marble Arch, W. 1, 262-1234 (910 rooms, all with baths). Huge and somewhat impersonal, but convenient for Oxford Street shopping. Garage. *£12 to £16.50. S. BNI.*

The Ebury Court, 24–32 Ebury Street, S.W. 1, 730-8147 (40 rooms, 8 with bath. Handy to Victoria, and Belgravia, small and pleasant. *£4.50 to £10.25. S.*

Europa, Grosvenor Square, W. 1, 493-1232 (289 rooms, all with baths). Practically next to the American Embassy, in the heart of Mayfair. *£10.50 to £16.*

The Goring, Grosvenor Gardens, S.W. 1, 834-8211 (87 rooms, all with baths). A good medium-sized hotel, very comfortable, moderate prices. *£10.50 to £16.*

The May Fair, Berkeley Street, W. 1, 629-7777 (400 rooms, all with private baths). A topflight hotel. *£11.50 to £18. S. 10%. BNI.*

The Mount Royal, Marble Arch, W. 1, 629-8040 (700 rooms, all with baths). Like the nearby Cumberland (see comments) but swankier. *£8.80 to £12.65. S. 10%.*

The Park Lane, Piccadilly, W. 1, 499-6321 (440 rooms, all with baths, including 40 suites with 2 baths). Luxurious and smart. Garage. *£9.90 to £15.50. S. 10%. BNI.*

The Piccadilly, Piccadilly and Regent Street, W. 1, 734-8000 (245 rooms, all with baths. Superb location for theaters, restaurants, shops. *£8.50 to £15. S. 10%.*

Meurice and Quaglino's, Bury St. S.W. 1, 930-6767 (41 rooms, all with bath). An excellent small hotel with a world-famous (and very expensive) restaurant. Garage. *£15 to £23.50. S. 10%. BNI.*

The Royal Court, Sloane Square, S.W. 1, 730-9191 (105 rooms, 76 with baths, plus 20 public baths). Charm and simple elegance. *£6 to £12. S. 10%.*

The Royal Lancaster, Lancaster Gate, W. 2, 262-6737 (433 rooms including 14 suites, all with private bath), new in 1967, is ultra-modern, extremely well located, with superb upper-floor views across Kensington Gardens and Hyde Park. *£10.35 to £17.25.*

Where to Stay

The Stafford, 16 St. James's Place, S.W. 1, 493-0111 (67 rooms, all with bath). Small, friendly, charming, expensive. £15 to £23. S. 15%. BNI.

The Strand Palace, The Strand, W.C. 2, 836-8080. Vast, central location, relatively inexpensive. (786 rooms, all with baths). £9.20 to £13.50. BNI.

The Stratford Court, 350 Oxford Street, W. 1, 629-7474 (135 rooms, all with baths). Moderate prices, convenient to shopping area. £9.72 to £15.60.

The Washington, Curzon Street, W. 1, 499-7030 (161 rooms, all with baths). Like the Westbury, for 100 per cent Americans. Good food, service, location. £8 to £11.50. S. 10%.

Good Hotels Outside the Center. Up to this point we have been concerned with hotels in the center of the city—the region of shops and theatres, of society and government. But London is considerably more spread out than Florence or Boston—more even than Paris or New York—and each of its outlying districts has its own peculiar flavor and attraction. After reading Chapter Five you may decide that you would like to stay in some specific non-central district: Chelsea, for instance, if you are interested in contemporary art and artists, or Holborn, near the British Museum, if you are a scholar, or residential areas like Kensington or Lancaster Gate if you happen to have English friends living there. Whatever your reason, these brief notes on hotel accommodations may be helpful.

The Kensington area south and west of Hyde Park contains a number of fine hotels, of which the following is a selection.

Blake's, 33 Roland Gardens, S.W. 7, 370-6071 (34 rooms with bath). A small, very chic hotel in the heart of Kensington. Popular with young entertainers. £9 to £13. BI, S. 15%.

The De Vere, 60 Hyde Park Gate, W. 8, 584-0051 (87 rooms, 78 with baths, plus 5 public bathrooms). Dignified Edwardian atmosphere. £7 to £15. S.

The Gore, 189 Queen's Gate, S.W. 7, 584-6601 (53 rooms, 48 with bath, plus 2 public baths). All facilities, good value. £4.25 to £9.

Kensington Close, Wright's Lane, W. 8, 937-8170 (540 rooms, all with baths). Small, compact rooms, but excellent location—a very good bargain. Garage. £9.50 to £16. S. BNI.

Kensington Palace, De Vere Gardens, W. 8, 937-8121 (300 rooms, all with baths). Almost palatial, as the name implies. £9.50 to £14. S.

Portobello, 22 Stanley Gardens, W. 11, 727-2777.

The Rembrandt, Thurloe Place, S.W. 7, 589-8100 (170 rooms, 75 with baths or showers). Pleasing atmosphere, emphasis on solid comfort. £4.80 to £10. S.

Here are some of the moderately priced hotels in the Kensington area. Although they do not have some of the facilities of the more expensive hotels, they are all clean and pleasant places.

The Glencourt, 42-45 Onslow Gardens, S.W. 7, 589-6242 (58 rooms, 36 with bath, 8 public baths). *£3.50 to £8.50. S.*
The Post House, 104/105 Bayswater Road, W. 2, 262-4461. (175 rooms, all with baths). Modern, overlooking Hyde Park. *£10 to £13.35.*
The Nat London, 147 Cromwell Road, 370-4341 (45 rooms, all with bath). Near West London Air Terminal. *£5.25 to £7.70.*

In the Bayswater-Lancaster Gate region north of Hyde Park the following hotels are recommended.

The Carlyle, 27 Devonshire Terrace, W. 2, 262-2204 (156 rooms, most with bath). Comfortable and relatively inexpensive. Garage. *£5.50 to £9. S.*
The Colonnade, 2 Warrington Crescent, W. 9, 286-1052 (40 rooms, 34 with bath or shower, plus 8 public baths). A good choice. *£4.50 to £12.*
The Great Western Royal, Paddington, W. 2, 723-8064 (175 rooms, 145 with baths, plus 8 public bathrooms). A large commercial hotel adjoining Paddington Station (British Railways' lines to the west). Garage. *£8.50 to £13. S. BNI.*
The Park Court, 75 Lancaster Gate, W. 2, 262-0121 (444 rooms, all with baths). Rather large, all facilities. Garage. *£8.50 to £13. S.*
White's, Lancaster Gate, W. 2, 262-2711 (70 rooms, all with baths). A good, quiet hotel overlooking Kensington Gardens. Garage. *£7.75 to £12.50. S. BNI.*

Less expensive hotels in this area are:

Arama, 44 Spring Street, W. 2, 262-5860 (28 rooms and 6 public bathrooms. *£5 to £8. S.*
Pembridge Court, 34 Pembridge Gardens, W. 2, 229-9977 (36 rooms, 15 with bath, plus 20 public showers). *£4.50 to £8. S.*
The Kensington Gardens, 84 Kensington Gardens, W. 2, 229-2913 (18 rooms, 2 with bath, 3 public baths). *Unlicensed. £4.50 to £8.50. S.*
King's, 62 Queensborough Terrace, 229-7055 (30 rooms, 11 with baths, 9 public baths). *Unlicensed. £3.75 to £7.50. S.*
The Pembridge Gardens, 1-9 Pembridge Gardens, W. 2, 229-5171 (100 rooms, 8 with baths, 15 public bathrooms). *£3.75 to £8. S.*
Royal Eagle, Craven Road, W. 2, 723-3202 (100 rooms, all with baths). *£6.50 to £10. S.*

Royal Albert Hall, one of London's great concert halls

Although the region east of Mayfair, comprising the City, the borough of Holborn, and Bloomsbury is more business and commercial than residential, there are a number of hotels in the area which deserve a listing.

The Bedford Corner, Bayley Street, W.C. 1, 580-7766 (84 rooms, 44 with baths, plus 8 public bathrooms). *£4.50 to £8.65. S.*
The Russell, Russell Square, W.C. 1, 837-6470 (328 rooms, most with bath). *£11 to £18. S.*
The Tavistock, Tavistock Square, W.C. 1, 636-8383 (302 rooms, all with baths. Garage. *£7.50 to £11 plus VAT, S.*

A Different Kind of Hotel. There are, in London, a surprising number of good hotels which do not offer a complete catering service, but which do provide breakfast. Most places of this type have no liquor license. As a group they tend to be small, clean, and comfortable—and to charge somewhat less than standard hotels for equivalent accommodations. While the BTA calls them "hotels not providing full meal service," the establishments themselves appear to be in some doubt as to whether the title properly applies to them, preferring, in some cases, to shelter behind such unspecific appelations as "Court" or "House," or simply an address. Many are, in fact, more like swank rooming houses than hotels. The services and facilities they provide vary widely, and these differences are reflected, generally speaking, in the prices they charge.

Unless otherwise noted, the establishments listed below are unlicensed. As before, the prices given are those of the cheapest single room without bath and the most expensive double with bath. In all

Whitehall, for many, the city's most exciting section

cases, breakfast is included in the prices given. In central London, the following are recommended:

Campden Court, 2 Basil Street, S.W. 3, 589-6286 (20 rooms, 12 with baths, plus 4 public bathrooms). *£6 to £12. S.*

Hansel and Gretel, 64–74 Belgrave Road, S.W. 1, 828-1806 (85 rooms, 25 public baths). *£4 to £6. S.*

Eaton Court, 85 Eaton Place, S.W. 1, 235-1152 (20 rooms, 10 with baths, plus 5 public baths). *£6 to £12. S.*

Gresham Hotel, 36 Bloomsbury Street, W.C. 1. Modest but reasonably priced pension near British Museum. *£3.50 to £7.00.*

Portman Court, 28 Seymour Street, W. 1, 402-5401 (30 rooms, 6 with baths, 6 public baths). *£2.50 to £6. S.*

Ryder Street Chambers, 3 Ryder St., S.W. 1, 930-3053 (10 suites, all with baths). Very comfortable. *£10 to £11.50. S. BNI.*

Willett, 32 Sloane Gardens, S.W. 1. (17 rooms, most with bath). Quiet but convenient to shopping. High standards. *£4.00 to £7.50.*

Of the numerous good places of the same kind in the Kensington area, the following are especially recommended:

Bolton Close, 300 Earl's Court Road, S.W. 5, 373-9511 (69 rooms, 21 with bath, plus 12 public baths). *£3.50 to £7.50. S.*

The French House, 71 Onslow Gardens, S.W. 7, 370-1075 (45 rooms, 3 with bath, 12 public baths). *£3.50 to £8.50. S.*

Diplomat, 2 Chesham Street, S.W. 1, 235-1544 (25 rooms with baths). *£5 to £9. S.*

Stanhope House, 59 Cromwell Road, S.W. 7, 373-0167 (24 rooms, all with bath). Newly renovated with elegant appointments. Priced correspondingly. *£8.50 to £25. S.*

The National Gallery

Furnished Apartments. If you are planning to stay in London for two weeks or longer and would like to keep living costs down, it will certainly be to your advantage to take a furnished apartment. The price of a "Bed-sitter" (i.e., a single room combining the functions of a bedroom and sitting room) either in what we would call a rooming house or in a private flat (apartment) or house, runs from about **£10 to about £20 a week, depending on the size and furnishings of the room and the desirability of its location, as well as the services provided.**

There are three standard methods of hunting for this kind of accommodations: (1) consulting the notice boards posted in the windows of shops in the neighborhood of your choice, (2) following up want ads in the local newspapers as well as in the *Evening Standard*, which appears on the stands at about 11 A.M. daily or *Time Out*, a weekly publication, and (3) taking your problem to one of the agencies that deal in furnished rooms.

As you probably won't have much time and certainly won't want to waste what time you have, the last course is recommended. Here, then, are the names, addresses, and telephone numbers of a few of the agencies which will, for a small fee, find you a suitable room—or even, in certain circumstances, the short-term lease of a flat.

The London Tourist Board, 4 Grosvenor Gardens, S.W. 1 (730-3400). A government service will steer you to the best agency for you, or you can buy their publication "Where to Stay in London" (15 p.) also available at their Victoria Station office on Platform 15 (open 9 to 9 every day).
London Accommodation Bureau, 309 Oxford St., N. 4 (359-5291). Furnished and unfurnished flats, bedsitters.
Jenny Jones Agency, 40 South Moulton St., W. 1 (493-4801/3783/0994). Flats and bedsitters and furnished houses.

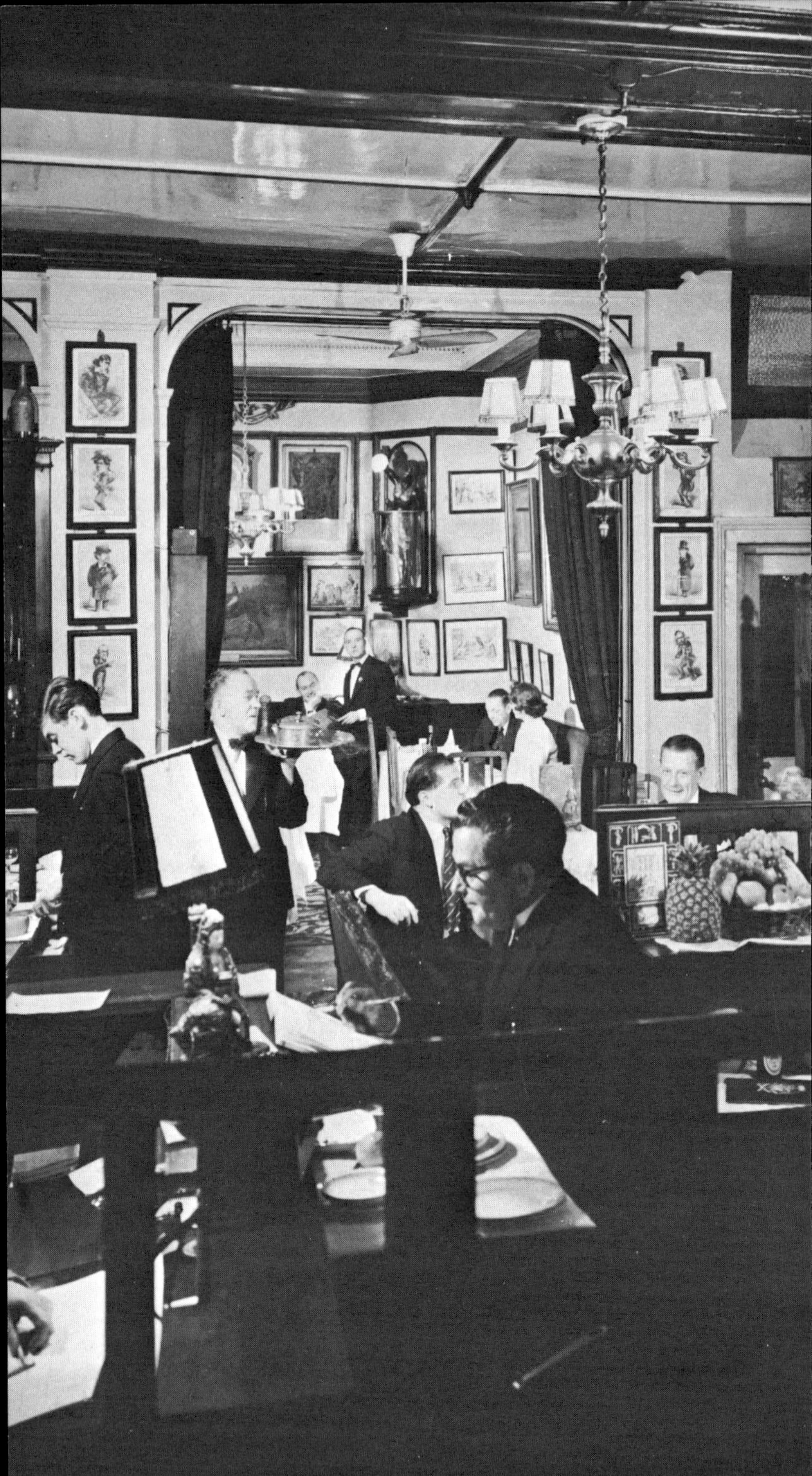

CHAPTER 7

WHERE TO EAT IN LONDON

Let's face it—London is not Paris. It hasn't nearly so many French restaurants. On the other hand, the British capital, like New York, San Francisco, and certain other American cities, is highly cosmopolitan in this regard: among its innumerable restaurants are represented the national foods of every country in Europe and of most of the rest of the world. You can even find English food here, though you may have to look for it.

Which brings us to English cooking. So many snide words have been printed and said on this subject, and for so long, that the resulting noise may have drowned out a significant piece of news: namely, that the island race has learned since the war to prepare food in a very adequate manner indeed. What's more, some of the Continent's finest chefs have been lured over by political upheavals in their homelands, by the thought of all the mouths to be properly fed, by bribes. So you can forget what Uncle Eustace says; the meals you get in London will be just as good as the ones Mother used to produce and may even be better.

Like everything else in London, the restaurants are scattered all over. The concentration is thickest in the neighborhood of theatres, a circumstance for which many a playgoer before you has been thankful. The unofficial "foreign quarter" of Soho is particularly rich in good spots. But because most hotels are situated to the west of this district, we'll begin our roundup in Mayfair. Incidentally, don't overlook the culinary potentialities of the big hotels: good food and service are, after all, two of their most important stocks in trade.

In the list that follows, expensive and inexpensive eating places

Rules, one of London's oldest and most famous restaurants

are indiscriminately mixed, the order being geographical first, alphabetical second. Unless some indication of price is given, you may assume that the tariff will be somewhere in the middle range—between, say, £3 and £6 ($6.00 and $12.00)—exclusive of tip. Generally speaking, prices are more or less the same than they are at home for everything except wine and other potables, which are taxed ferociously by the government. Tip as you would in America.

Finally, a word to the wise. Book your table in advance (telephone numbers in the directories) to be sure that it isn't cook's night out and that there's room for you. And now, as they say in Merrie England, *Bon appetit!*

MAYFAIR

The Café Royal, 68 Regent Street, W.1, is, *per contra*, spacious, and, as the name suggests, regal. Formerly the haunt of O. Wilde, J. Whistler & Co., it is rich with ripe old nostalgia. Dinner about £6.50.

Cunningham's, 17b Curzon Street, W.1, has an intimate, dark atmosphere that is luxurious and very English: the menu is even printed in that language. A justly famous oyster bar. Expensive.

The Guinea, 30 Bruton Place, W.1 (off Berkeley Square), offers basic fare of a generous slab of beef plus salad. On entering, you takes your choice (from vast chunks of meat on display) and before leaving you pays your money—a lot of it. Popular with Americans!

Martinez, 25 Swallow Street, W.1, is Spanish. The sherries are great, and the wines, by English standards, remarkably cheap. Dinner a bargain at about £3.

The Mirabelle, 56 Curzon Street, W.1, has the best of everything, but you have to pay for it. Haunt of rich industrialists and veteran movie stars. The wines are superb. So is the service. So (especially) is the garden restaurant, open in summer. High prices.

ST. JAMES

Fortnum & Masons, 181 Piccadilly, W.1. A lunchtime bargain if you can get into this sunny, pleasant tea-room/soda fountain. Delicious salads, pastries, milk shakes. A favorite with shoppers and children.

Overton's, 5 St. James Street, S.W.1, provides hard-to-beat sea food and grills, middays and evenings. Cozy, quiet atmosphere.

Pruniers, 72 St. James's Street, S.W.1, is the London branch of the Paris institution whose reputation among gourmets is *mondial.* Everything from the sea. Haddock Soufflé a specialty, but *not* quick service.

The Hard Rock Café, 150 Old Park Lane, W. 1. An American highway café with waitresses in '30's gear. Delicious hamburgers, club sandwiches, salads, thick shakes. Inexpensive.

SOHO

The Braganza, 56 Frith Street, is in the *Wheelers* chain of restaurants, and serves high quality fish dishes, prepared in a wide variety of ways. Rather expensive.

Chez Gérard, 5 Charlotte Street, W. 1. Excellent French Grille in an easy, informal atmosphere with a background of jazz. Dinner about £3.

Where to Eat in London

Escargot Bienvenu, 48 Greek Street, W.1, is again very French, and certain Londoners who ought to know claim it's the best restaurant in town. Wonderful old waiters, first-class ground-floor wine "cellar," caricatures from the Edwardian era.

L'Etoile, 30 Charlotte Street, W.1, is old fashioned, bustling and very French. A haunt for publishers and other regulars despite cook's occasional off days. Dinner about £6.

Lacy's, 26 Whitfield Street, W. 1. A superb chef and his gourmet wife chair this popular restaurant. Original dishes; dinner about £5.

Chuen Cheng Ku, 17/23 Wardour Street, W. 1. This very reasonable restaurant in the heart of Chinatown treats you to local color as well as to delicious dumplings, shrimps in rice paper and special fried rice. At its most jumping for Sunday lunch.

La Terrazza, 19 Romilly Street, W. 1. The first of the famous swinging sixties "trattorias." Owners have kept the standards high and the noise level, too. Good place to see celebrities and eat good Italian cuisine. Dinner about £5.

Scott's, 20 Mount Street, W. 1, is just the place for a lavish post-theater wingding. Incomparable food and service—and expensive.

Wheelers, 19 Old Compton Street, W.1, is *the* oyster house of London, where you can also get lobsters and salmon in season. The tone is smart, and if you are able to spot them when they are not sporting their coronets, you may spy a titled couple or two at nearby tables.

The White Tower, 17 Percy Street, W.1, is Greek, and also one of the best restaurants in London. Moussaka, stuffed vine leaves, and the best possible retsina. Also international dishes. A hang-out of World War II newspaper correspondents. Dinner about £6.

Coffee al fresco in Shepherd Market

South of Soho

Boulestin, 25 Southampton Street, W.C.2, is elaborate, ornate and very good. Monsieur Boulestin campaigned long and tirelessly for the elevation of British feeding standards, and though he is now unfortunately gone, his spirit, gastronomically speaking, lives on in his timeless temple. More nostalgia present than other customers. Be ready to donate generously.

The Ivy, 1 West Street, W.C.2, is one of London's most distinguished restaurants. A gathering place for theater people, who set the tone: sophisticated, international. Dinner about £3.50 pre-theatre; more later.

Rules, 35 Maiden Lane, W.C.2, is a place you really should visit to see what all the shouting is about. Dickensian atmosphere, Edwardian cartoons, ceiling fans, skylight. The fare is very English . . . with all that implies. Dinner about £4.

Sheekey's Fish Restaurant, 29 St. Martin's Court, Charing Cross Road, W.C.2, frequently has more than its share of stage notables who have drifted in from the theaters roundabout. Stewed eel (good!)

Simpson's, 100 Strand, W.C.2, is universally acknowledged to possess the highest standards in a field in which English claims to supremacy have never been disputed: to wit, the preparation of roasts and joints. The beef and mutton here are famous. Beer served in pewter mugs, wine list excellent and amazingly reasonable for London.

Belgravia

Marcel, 14 Sloane Street, S.W.1, can set a memorable dish before you on your scrubbed wooden table. Try, especially, his steak. Dinner about £6.

Le Gavroche, 61–63 Lower Sloane Street, S.W. 1. The hautest of London's haute cuisine and unquestionably London's best French restaurant. Dinner about £8 *not* including wine.

Le Perroquet, Berkeley Hotel, Wilton Place, S.W. 1. Offers one of the best luncheon buffets in the city. For about £3 you can eat as much as you want from the cold spread plus one hot dish and dessert.

The Belfry, 11b West Halkin Street, S.W. 1. Once a well-attended Presbyterian Church, this restaurant was the scene of Prince Philip's bachelor dinner in 1947. Very unusual. Dinner about £6.

Chelsea

Artiste Affamé (the Hungry Artist!), 243 Old Brompton Road, S.W. 5, has French cuisine and charming décor, using part of an old carousel. Excellent service, young crowd. Closed Sundays. Medium price.

Au Père de Nico, 10 Lincoln Street, S.W.3 (almost in Knightsbridge), is the favorite London bistro of quite a number of discriminating people. Brightly colored tablecloths and ditto posters; enchanting whitewashed courtyard in the rear for both summer and winter dining. Dinner about £5.

The Casserole, 338 King's Road, S.W.3, has French cuisine with a Mediterranean accent. Very trendy but casual, and the bill will be about £4.

Verbanella, 30 Beauchamp Place, S.W. 3, has good, moderately priced Italian cuisine, reasonable wines.

Don Luigi, 33c King's Road, S.W. 3. Popular, lively Italian restaurant whose desserts have become locally famous. Try the zabaglione. £3.

World's End One, 1A Langton Street, Kings Road, S.W. 10, in the *world's end* section of Chelsea, has cellar and main floor intimate dining, on health-conscious French and international food. Moderate.

Chelsea Rendezvous, 4 Sydney Street, S.W. 3. New, pretty, fashionable Chinese restaurant where the clientèle is fresh from the pages of fashion magazines. About £4.

Where to Eat in London

SOUTH KENSINGTON

Bangkok, 14 Bute Street, S.W. 7, offers Siamese food in a small, cozy setting. Sate and spare ribs especially good; students and artists like their moderate prices (£3).

Star of India, 154 Old Brompton Rd., S.W. 5. One of London's many Indian restaurants, many of them delicious and really inexpensive. This one boasts excellent kebabs and bhajias as well as a faithful clientèle. Dinner about £2.

The Elizabethan Room next door to the Gore Hotel, 190 Queens Gate, S.W.7, whisks you back four centuries to the reign of the first Elizabeth. Rushes on the floor, wooden platters to eat from, serving wenches to observe by candlelight. Boar's head, peacock and syllabub to eat; claret, mead and ale to drink; £2.50 (about $5.00) to pay.

KENSINGTON

The Alcove, 17 Kensington High Street, W. 8. Small, cozy and intimate with red velvet/wood panelled atmosphere. Good place to relax and eat for reasonable prices.

Chinese Lantern, 4 Thackeray Street, W. 8. This bambooed and paper lanterned spot is very popular for family parties or couples who want a long time to sit. The set dinner menu has 8 or 9 courses, all excellent, and costs about £4. Plenty of atmosphere.

MARYLEBONE

Angus Steak House, 5 Blandford Street, W.1, supplies the Scotch variety of steak in profusion. The T-bone and rump steaks are recommended for flavor.

Today's ideas about 16th century eating and entertainment are featured at the Elizabethan Room.

CITY CHOPHOUSES

As in New York, some of the best eating places in London are hidden away in the financial district, where businessmen forgather at lunchtime. The chophouses of the old City of London generally began their existence a good long time ago as taverns, and have remained such to this day. In general, they are distinguished by a minimum of decorative froufrou and a maximum of plain masculine comfort. The food is good, simple and cheap. Space forbids detailed descriptions, but at any of the places listed hereunder you can absorb a bit of London history with your lunch at no extra charge.

Ye Olde Cheshire Cheese, Wine Office Court, 145 Fleet Street, E.C.4. Sawdust on the floor, clay pipes in pots on the window sills. A bit self-conscious, but a must for antiquarians. Most famous Olde Englishe Inne in town.

The Cock Tavern, 22 Fleet Street, E.C.4. Original tavern was known to Pepys, Dickens and Tennyson. Note the cock sign carved by Grinling Gibbons.

The George & Vulture, 3 Castle Court, E.C.3. Chaucer knew it as The George. Pickwick's London headquarters. First-rate chophouse fare.

Throgmorton, Throgmorton Street, E.C.2. Lunch à la carte from 12:00 to 3:00. Closed weekends.

Simpson's Tavern, Ball Court, 38½ Cornhill, E.C.3. Ground-floor grill room; crowd almost wholly made up of City types.

Ye Olde Watling, Watling Street, E.C. 4. Said to be the oldest; built just after the Great Fire, was a refreshment station for Wren's workmen for decades thereafter. The front room has hand-hewn beams, Hogarth prints, copper pots.

Ye Olde Cheshire Cheese has treats for all palates.

Where to Eat in London

EATING ON THE CHEAP

Unlike Paris, London abounds in places where one can have a quick, nourishing meal for very little. By little we mean 80 p. ($1.60) for a main course (including meat), dessert, and tea or coffee. If you want less, you can have it for less. Needless to say, your wiener schnitzel won't be cooked in brandy, but you won't suffer any unpleasant after-effects, either. Such popular items of the English diet as pork pie, chips, flans of various sorts, etc., may be a bit starchy for your taste, but there are enough alternatives available these days to permit you to avoid them.

Don't bother to search in Mayfair or Belgravia, but anywhere else in central London you will easily find cheap restaurants or cafés in the side streets. Menus are usually posted in the windows. Most are owned and run by a family. The main perceptible difference between the two categories is that restaurants provide tablecloths while cafés do without. Incidentally, the cherished middle-class belief that working-class people pronounce café "kaff" is without foundation; they say "kaffy."

There are two vast chains of cafeterias covering the metropolis— **Jolyon** and the **A.B.C.** (Aerated Bread Company). Both also sell bakery products.

In recent years, snack bars and milk bars on the American model have been opening up in great numbers. The leading names in this field are Forte and the Golden Egg. But perhaps the most spectacular change in the eating habits of London's millions has been the triumph of that humble adjunct to gracious living—the hamburger. Fantastic as it may seem, J. Wellington Wimpy of the *Popeye* strip ("I'll gladly pay you Tuesday for a hamburger today") is more widely memorialized in London today than, for example, the Duke of Wellington. **Wimpy Bars** (a trade name) are everywhere.

And aside from the Wimpy version of a hamburger, London has recently been besieged with the real thing as well: several "American-Style" hamburger (chicken, barbecued spare ribs, etc.) "heavens" as well. **The Hard Rock Café,** 150 Old Park Lane, W.1 offers the real thing as well as shakes and sodas, fudge cake, B.L.T.'s and club sandwiches in a small town U.S.A. setting with football pennants, pin-ball machines, and ceiling fans. The Hilton Hotel has a **Tavern** also serving big hamburgers, and there are two places named **Great American Disaster** (9 Beauchamp Place, S.W. 3, and 335 Fulham Road, S.W. 10) which probably win the prize both for hamburgers and decibels (Pop and Rock). Children love them all.

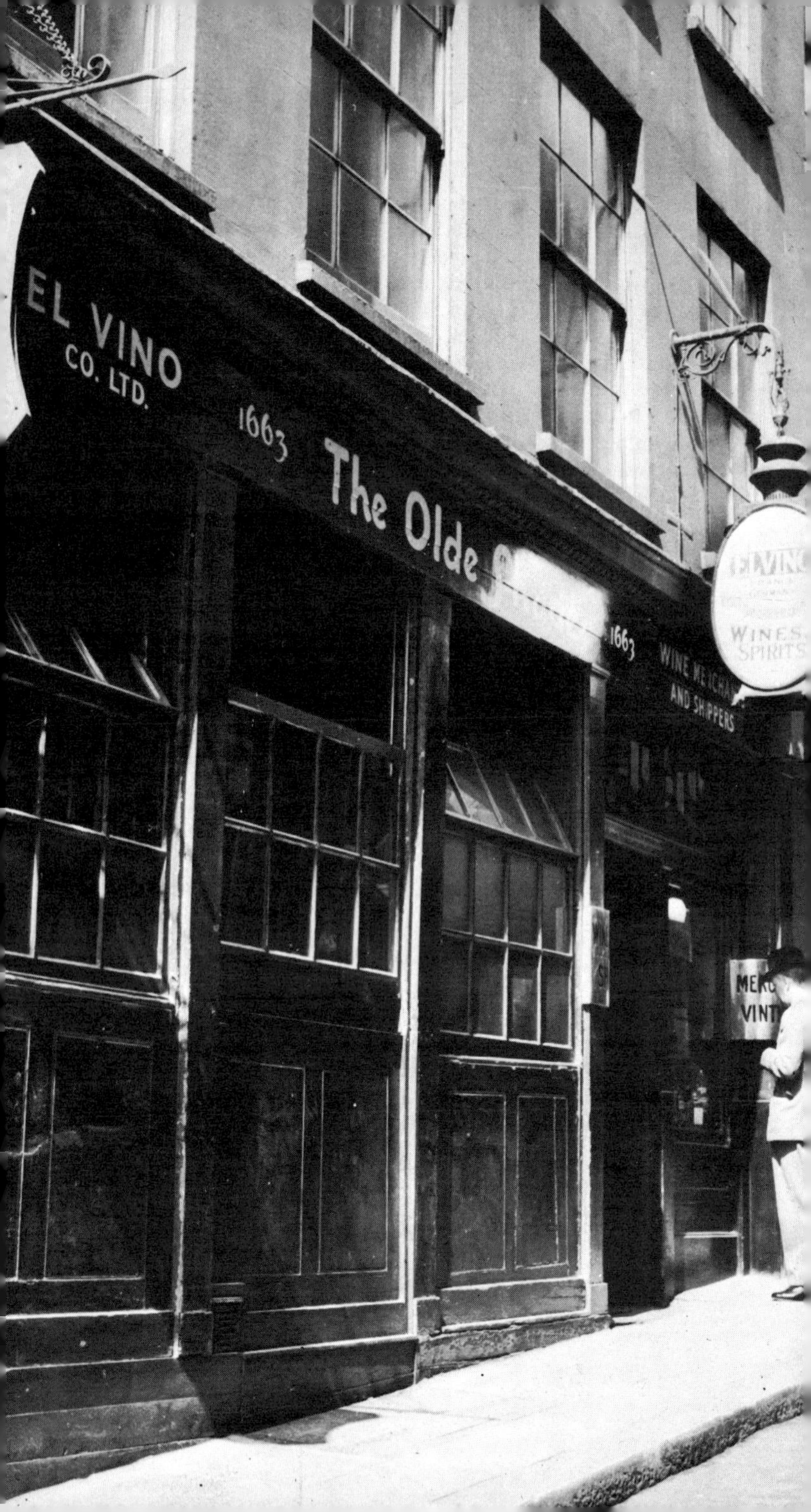
EL VINO
CO. LTD.
1663
The Olde
1663
AND SHIPPERS
WINES,
SPIRITS

CHAPTER 8

PUBS AND WINE HOUSES

ABOUT PUBS

As everybody knows, many an Englishman prefers his pub to his home. Even if the latter still is his castle, the former is his club, which is cozier, jollier and more stimulating. So much has been written in praise of the institution that more would be superfluous at this point —if pub-drinking were not such a fundamentally different proposition from dropping around to the corner bar for a quick one.

Most Londoners cherish their "locals," but the most dedicated will cheerfully admit (if they don't angrily allege) that the laws restricting public consumption of alcoholic beverages to certain hours of the day and night are maddening, tyrannical, and outmoded, though they've been relaxed by a recent revision. The men and women behind the bar don't concur; they contend that if other people have a right to a working day of eight or nine hours, they do too. This argument, to be fair, has more force in Britain, with its multiplicity of small family-run enterprises.

Whatever the merits of the opposing viewpoints, the fact remains that the majority of pubs in London are open only from 11:00 to 3:00 and from 5:30 to 11:00 Monday through Saturday, and from 12:00 noon to 2:00 and from 7:00 to 10:30 on Sunday. A handful of places have special arrangements which enable them to stay open at other times, for the convenience of travelers or of people working at specific off-hour jobs (e.g., the porters at Covent Garden). In a specially designated West End area, clubs, restaurants, and hotels can serve you until 3:00 A.M. *if* they have music and dancing.

As to the pubs themselves, they furnish endless material for speculations on the British character, the ways of Londoners and the nature of the neighborhoods in which they are located. Americans

The pub's first cousin—a London wine Shop

visiting Britain for the first time are invariably surprised to discover that most pubs are firmly divided into two compartments, separated from each other by a wall, each with its own entrance from the street. These are, as the signs announce, the public bar and the saloon bar. The first (from which "pub" is derived) used to be drab and sparsely decorated while the second was inviting, fully or overly furnished, and throned with jovial and talkative customers who were perfectly happy to be spending a penny or two extra for the same beer that is sold on the other side of the wall for less. These distinctions have become increasingly blurred over the years; in fact nowadays, it's considered "in" to be working class—or at least to pretend to be!

ABOUT PUB DRINKING

The basic tipple of Londoners, as of Britishers generally, is beer—sold on draught, in bottles, and (in a few places) in cans. Bitter and mild are the main types of draught brew, and neither resembles the American beer "on tap" in the slightest. Bitter is heavily hopped and normally the strongest; it comes as a rule in two categories, "best" and "ordinary." A recommended first step for the tyro is to sample a half pint of the former by asking for "a half of best bitter." It will be served at room temperature, of course, and probably in a cut-glass stein. Mild ale is sweeter, darker and cheaper. Mild and bitter, also called "half and half," is a mixture of the two.

Both bitter and mild are available almost everywhere, but certain other draught brews may require a search. Guinness, a rich and potent stout, is sold mainly in free houses and in all "Irish houses." Scotch ale is a dark bitter, found chiefly in pubs of the Younger chain. Burton, or old, is sweet, very dark, and sold only in the north.

The brands of bottled beer stocked by a given pub depend on the proprietor's commercial allegiances. Practically all houses carry Guinness and two leading pale ales, Bass and Worthington. In addition they can provide a best pale ale, a light ale, a darker and sweeter pale ale called brown ale, a stout, and a lager. The last, a lightly hopped beer, closely resembles American beer in taste. It is always served cold. Most pub owners have taken to installing a "chilled beer service" for the rest of their line. Once again, this innovation has aroused the scorn of discriminating regulars, who hold that refrigeration ruins the taste of everything except lager.

You won't be eyed askance if you ask for something else in the way of a light drink—a glass of wine, for instance. Cider is good, too, and sometimes available from the cask; of the various brands, Merrydown is reputedly the strongest. And of course you can get whiskey (meaning Scotch), gin, brandy, rum, and a host of other liquors and liqueurs. The most popular spirituous drink in London pubs is probably gin-and-tonic; other favorites are gin-and-lime juice and Pimm's

Pubs and Wine Houses 99

Cup. If you crave a dry martini (unknown in some places and confused in others with something called gin-and-French), you will be well advised to take over the preparation thereof—unless you like yours two parts vermouth to one of gin. If you're addicted to bourbon, you'd better stick to the bars of the big West End hotels. Finally, you may, perhaps, rejoice to hear that the British have at long last come to accept, and even, grudgingly, to welcome, the presence of ice in their long drinks.

THE RESIDENTIAL WEST END

The Antelope, Eaton Terrace, S.W.1. Much favored by the post-debutantes of Belgravia and their dashing escorts, who can be seen on most summer evenings crowding the sidewalk out front. Inside, the atmosphere is in the best traditions of pubdom. Good restaurant upstairs.

The Grenadier, Wilton Row, S.W.1. This is the "local" of the mews village that surrounds it, completely isolated from the noise and bustle of Knightsbridge. Pub connoisseurs delight in its unspoiled appearance, outside and in.

The Red Lion, 2 Duke of York Street, S.W.1. A fine example of the Victorian "gin palace" with mirrored walls, a cast iron staircase and a horseshoe shaped bar.

The Nag's Head, 53 Kinnerton Street, S.W.1. A small and intimate example of the mews ale-shop.

Shepherds Tavern, 50 Hertford Street, Mayfair W. 1, is a pub-restaurant in the middle of Shepherd Market. Upstairs are old fireplaces and chandeliers, antique tables, and full menus of traditional English food. A sedan chair plays the role of telephone booth!

The Star Tavern, Belgrave Mews West, S.W.1. Still another delightful mews pub, where you can sit outside and observe the placid, decorous life of a self-contained (and exceedingly well-off) community.

Nearer to Berkeley Square in Mayfair are many pleasant, lively pubs.

The Audley, 41 Mount Street, W.1 is an enormous Victorian spot, usually packed, but somehow there's always room for one more. Great atmosphere.

Barley Mow, 82 Duke Street, W.1. Another Victorian pub, this time with a farm feeling—horse brasses and leather. Hot and cold snacks upstairs.

The Guinea, 30 Bruton Place, W.1. A pub that's been there forever—well, for 600 years. Hot lunches and snacks at the bar; expensive grills in the two small dining rooms.

MAINLY AROUND THE THEATRES

The Nag's Head, 10 James Street, W.C. 2. Once the most raucous pub in Covent Garden; now that the market is closed it is still well filled in the evenings before ballet or opera.

The Dog and Duck, Bateman Street, W.1. Interesting especially for its clientele, among whom are many avant garde artists.

Lamb, Lamb's Conduit Street, W.C.1. With its Edwardian photographs and decor, this is a place where painters and poets congregate.

The Lamb and Flag, Rose Street, W.C.2 (just off the street named for England's greatest thespian, Garrick). Usually shelters a high quota of present-day actors, working and "at liberty."

Mooney's Irish House, 395 Strand, W.C.2. A place where Irishmen, whether from Boston or Baile-atha-Cliath, will feel thoroughly at home.

The Museum Tavern, opposite the British Museum in Great Russell Street, W.C.1. Patronized by students and intellectuals.

Rayners, Haymarket, S.W.1. Another up-to-date pub whose location just off Piccadilly Circus makes it an ideal place to rendezvous with friends. Complete buffet, if you want lunch or a snack.

The Salisbury, St. Martin's Lane, W.C.2. Is likewise much frequented by stage folk. It is one of the relatively few remaining London pubs which retain the full glitter and solidity of the "gin palace" of the eighties and nineties.

The Samuel Whitbread, Leicester Square, W.2. Outlines the shape of things to come. Vast picture windows allow the customers to be seen from the street, thus defying the puritan equating of drinking with evil. Excellent English restaurant.

The Sherlock Holmes, a few steps away from Charing Cross in Northumberland Street, W.C.2. A must for people who savor childhood memories of the great sleuth. In addition to a rich collection of Holmesiana on walls and windows, there is, upstairs, the lovingly reconstructed living room of 221B Baker Street.

The York Minster, Dean Street, W.1. The meeting place for London's permanent French colony; has a fine French restaurant up one flight.

The Salisbury, full splendor of the 19th century pub

Pubs and Wine Houses

THE CITY

For obvious reasons, City pubs tend to be heavily patronized during the lunch hour and the evening rush hours, and then so thoroughly deserted that they shut up shop at about 7:00. Following are a few of the many good places.

The Black Friar, 174 Queen Victoria Street, E.C.4. Has a great deal of copper, stained glass, mosaic and marble inside and out, and has been hailed as London's best arts and crafts pub.

The Castle, Cowcross Street, E.C.1. Notable for the fact that it is also a pawnshop, an earlier landlord having been granted a pawnbroker's license by George IV.

Cheshire Cheese, 145 Fleet Street, E.C.4. Described on page 94.

Dirty Dick's, 202 Bishopsgate, E.C.2. This very old pub is named for the original owner, a famous boozer, and must look very much as it did years ago with stained glass windows and bare boards. The basement is in the original wine vaults.

Railway Tavern, 15 Liverpool Street, E.C.2. A monument to the steam engine, the decor includes model trains, crests of railway companies and notices of regulations.

The Ship Tavern, 3 Hart Street at Mark Lane, E.C.3. Enjoys a distinct "personality" which owes much to the proximity of Leadenhall Market.

EAST END AND DOWN THE RIVER

Some of London's most fascinating pubs are situated in the grimy slums of the East End and the grim, forbidding heart of Dockland. They are mostly small, with one bar only (the public, of course). Places along the river have balconies hanging out over the mud flats, from which you can watch the ships go by, some bound for far distant ports.

The first two below are on the south bank, the remainder on the north bank or inland from it.

The Anchor, Bankside, S.E.1. The last remaining Bankside pub. It is Georgian and quite perfect except for the new decorations. Among other curious features, it has a concealed shaft giving access to a tiny room in which convicts escaping from nearby "Clink" prison could purchase temporary sanctuary.

The Mayflower, 117 Rotherhithe Street, S.E.16. A tiny and quite unspoiled chunk of the early 19th century. Balcony view of the river.

The Grapes, Narrow Street, E.14. A minute place, with sawdust on the floor of front and back rooms. The latter leads to a tiny balcony from which the barges look startlingly large and near.

The Gun, 27 Coldharbour, E.14. On the Isle of Dogs. Victorian and cozy, it commands a superb eastward view of Blackwell Reach. Watch the ships go by on their way to the West India Dock.

The Prospect of Whitby, 57 Wapping Wall, E.1. One of those places everybody says you must see because the other tourists don't. Actually, it's about as far off the beaten track as Piccadilly Circus. Even so it's worth a visit for the fantastically eclectic curios, the carefully cultivated atmosphere of skulduggery, and the splendid view of Limehouse Reach.

CHELSEA, KENSINGTON, AND NORTH

Whether or not the large incidence of writers among the local population has anything to do with it, Chelsea has several good pubs within easy stride of one another. Sunday between the hours of 12:00 and 2:00 is the best time to observe how the pubs function in the community—and vice versa.

The Cross Keys, Lawrence Street, S.W.3. Small, intimate and charming.

The King's Head and Eight Bells, 50 Cheyne Walk, S.W.3. Enjoys the patronage of social and artistic types, mostly young, some of them locals and some of whom zoom up in their sports cars for the fun. In fine weather you carry your drink outside into the leafy public garden. If you cross the road, you can see the river swans stomping around in the mud at low tide, looking uncomfortably like the crowd you've left behind.

Bunch of Grapes, 207 Brompton Road, S.W. 3. Beautiful mid-Victorian decorations on doors, windows and glass partitions.

Along Chelsea's main drag, the King's Road, you have a number of pubs to choose from. Recommended are the **Chelsea Potter**, cheerful and inviting, the **Roebuck** at no. 354 where local artists sell their paintings and the **Duke of Cumberland,** further on (235 New King's Road), a beautifully restored Victorian pub.

The Anglesea, Selwood Terrace, S.W.7. Has space out front for drinking and socializing in fine weather. A small and unpretentious free house, it bears few marks of the 20th century.

The King's Arms (popularly known as "Finch's"), 190 Fulham Road, S.W.10. Remarkable for two things: the splendor of its unreconstructed Victorian interior and the extraordinary number of beards displayed by its customers (many of whom belong to the black windbreaker and blue jeans school of as-yet-undiscovered geniuses).

The Windsor Castle, Campden Hill, W.8. Has a "country" feeling about it. The walled garden through the "sherry" bar (saloon bar) has quite unsynthetic charm.

Even if you're not staying anywhere near Paddington you ought to look in at the **Victoria Tavern,** 10A Strathearn Place, W.2. As perfectly realized a Victorian reconstruction as any in London, guaranteed to induce affable sentiments in the sourest of souls. The Theatre Bar upstairs is a red-plush masterpiece with seats and boxes from the old Gaiety Theatre; and the small dining room might have come straight from a Georgian country house. As a matter of fact, it did.

In Marylebone, finally, you will be well advised not to hurry past the **Dover Castle** in Weymouth Mews, W.1, which, like the Victoria, is a haunt of entertainment-world celebrities. Its atmosphere can only be described, rather feebly, as original: a tank of fish on the counter, log seats, a display of glass, and antlers to hang your coat on. Drinks are sold there, too.

WINE HOUSES

Though Britain has never been a wine-growing country, it is instructive to remember that Chaucer, Shakespeare and Co. drank Continental wines in London taverns. The tradition of the city's wine houses is therefore of tolerably long standing, and their dominating feature—rows of vast wooden casks—is the same as it has always been. Wine is sold by the glass, and most wine houses serve snacks, sandwiches, salads and sometimes substantial meals. Many wine bars are owned by importers and wholesalers of wine, and will have an "off licence" show next door where you can buy your preference by the bottle. Some of the best places are listed below, all but three of them in the City. (Like pubs in that area, they tend to shut down early, and they close on Saturdays and Sundays.)

The Capataz, 89 Old Broad Street, E.C.2. Rather like a French wine *cave*, with sawdust on the floor, a long counter, and barrels for tables.

W. Coates, 109 Old Broad Street, E.C.2. Seems remarkably sober-minded for a drinking place, with unsmiling gentlemen in dark suits tending the casks. Mahogany and green baize décor.

El Vino, 47 Fleet Street, E.C.4. More relaxed, being patronized principally by journalists rather than businessmen. Ladies are not allowed to stand at the bar and are gently pushed away from the scene of (verbal) battle.

Emberson's Wine and Oyster Bar, in Mayfair, 56 Shepherd Street. W. 1. Will provide you with oysters in season or smoked salmon to eat with the wine you drink at the barrel tables. One of the "free vintners."

Balls Bros., Moor House, Moorfields, E.C.2, offers about 20 wines, including sherries and ports. Balls also has snacks and meals.

The Loose Box, 7 Cheval Place, S.W.7. In a pretty mews just across the street from Harrods, this wine bar has delicious salads and cold plates.

Cork & Bottle, 44 Cranbourn Street, W.C.2 is a very crowded, popular spot with a wide variety of excellent cold food.

For Beauty
MAX FACTOR
MON CHÉRI
COMMERCIAL UNION ASSURANCE

CHAPTER 9

ENTERTAINMENT AND NIGHTLIFE

This chapter might be called "London After Dark"—except that such a title would be quite misleading. In summer, at any rate, the big business of entertaining the city's inhabitants and visitors gets into high gear long before the Mayfair sun sinks into the Serpentine. The reason for this is threefold. London, sharing a parallel of latitude with Labrador, has shorter nights than any place in the United States south of Alaska. British Standard Time permanently adds an extra hour of day to the evening. And the custom of ringing up the curtain at 7:30 or thereabouts, adopted during the war, has persisted since. The result is that it only starts to get dark about midway through the second act, if then.

Most Londoners go to bed early, between 10 and 11. Does this mean that night owls are out of luck? Not at all: there are plenty of roosts where you can perch until the wee hours and even the not-so-wee ones. When these places shut down there is always Covent Garden, with its fascinating early morning bustle.

Theatres. The vitality of the London stage, the excellence of its actors, and the high quality of its productions need no elaboration. Plays are, like other attractions, advertised daily in all the papers, and briefly described in that invaluable weekly entertainment guide, *What's On in London* or the newer and trendier *Time Out* magazine. Tickets (at prices that are low by Broadway standards) can be obtained through your hotel or a ticket agent or direct from the box office. The orchestra is known as the stalls, the balcony as the dress circle, the second balcony as the balcony. Tea is generally served during intermissions (called intervals), and most theatres have one or more bars open at such times for thirstier patrons. Programs

Piccadilly circus—hub of the theater and shopping districts

(programmes) cost 10 to 50p. You are not expected to tip the lady usher who shows you to your seat, but you *are* expected to stand in silence (not necessarily at attention) during the playing of the National Anthem, which may take place before the curtain rises or immediately after the last curtain call.

In addition to the famous legitimate West End theatres there are certain other playhouses, usually smaller, which present experimental productions, including the work of new writers. The most important are the *Royal Court Theatre*, Sloane Square, S.W.1 and the *Theatre Royal*, Stratford, E.15, which charges only a little more for seats than most movie houses. The newest is the *Mermaid* at Puddle Dock, E.C.4, the City's first theatre in 250 years.

Vaudeville. Vaudeville (usually called variety or pantomime) survives in London, though it has been badly hit by competition from television. Main theatres are the huge *Palladium* and the big *Palace*.

Concerts, Opera and Ballet. London is, of course, one of the great world centers for music and allied arts. Concerts and recitals of every description are put on throughout the year. See *This Month In London,* the *Observer* and *Sunday Times*, or the London afternoon papers. London's Carnegie Hall is still the vast Albert Hall, in Kensington, though the Bankside complex of the Royal Festival Hall and the new Queen Elizabeth Hall and Purcell Room, is now *the* place for symphony concerts and recitals.

The Covent Garden Opera House and the Coliseum Theatre in St. Martin's Lane, the home of the Sadler's Wells company are the two big places for opera in central London. The former is also the home of the Royal Ballet company, but it specializes in opera in original languages with international casts. Sadler's Wells performs opera and operetta in English; it is the nursery of English opera singers.

Buskers. While you are queueing (standing in line) for seats at some attraction you may be treated to some energetic entertainment by buskers, singly or in pairs. These characters, practitioners of an

Famous old theatres: Covent Garden and the Haymarket

Entertainment and Nightlife

ancient profession, include singers, instrumentalists, jugglers, tumblers, clowns, and sleight-of-hand artists, and a number of them are surprisingly good. You can show (or withhold) your appreciation when the hat comes your way.

AFTER THE SHOW

What to do after the play (musical, concert, opera, ballet, movie)? Well, if you've only had a snack beforehand the chances are you'll want dinner. Many restaurants will be ready to serve you (after all, it's still this side of 11:00), including a generous smattering of the ones mentioned in the chapter on restaurants.

If you feel like combining the pleasures of the dance floor with those of the table, there is no dearth of places to meet your wish. Some have plain and fancy floor shows, or cabarets, as well. Evening dress is hardly ever required anywhere these nights, although a reasonably sober style of dress is advisable, particularly in the smarter establishments. Most London nightspots have bars which open early in the evening. Most serve theatre dinners until about 8:00. And all must conform with the licensing laws by cutting off the liquor supply at 3:00 a.m.

After-dark hangouts fall into two convenient categories. The hotels and restaurants, firstly, feature food, drink, music, soft lights, and "family-type" entertainment, more or less in that order. Then there are the night clubs proper . . . and improper. Unlike their transatlantic counterparts, however, they actually are clubs, or semblances thereof, in order to get around puritanical legal strictures on certain aspects of merry-making. Unless you are the guest of a member you will have to join to get in. Membership costs from £1.50 to £15. In fact now (as always in theory) you must wait at least 48 hours after applying before you can use a club, but more liberal liquor laws for West End restaurants and hotels have made the clubs less important to drop-in visitors in search of liquid refreshment.

From 11 p.m., when the pubs close, London's life centers around Mayfair. The lists that follow cannot pretend to comprehensiveness any more than the ones given earlier in this book, but you should certainly find a place here to suit your mood. Generally speaking prices in the hotels and restaurants are slightly lower than in the U.S., and in the night clubs somewhat higher. As used here this term includes certain "clubs" (i.e., private restaurants and bars) which are open during nightclubbing hours as well as earlier. Tipping is not discouraged. The shield indicates that the American Express Credit Card is honored.

DINING AND DANCING

The Dorchester, Park Lane, W.1 is lush but not exorbitant. Dinner-dancing from 8:00 to 1:00. Sedate atmosphere. A la carte menu runs about £7.50. No cabaret.
Celebrity, 13 Clifford Street, New Bond Street, W. 1. Cabaret twice nightly (10:30, 11:30). Minimum with dinner (French food) £5.50. Closed Sundays. 8:30–4:00.
The Hilton Rooftop Restaurant, Park Lane, W.1. Dinner and dancing from 9:00 P.M., Monday through Saturday. Dancing continues until 1:00 A.M. The menu is extremely expensive (£7 minimum). No cabaret, but two excellent dance bands, one usually a pop group, perform in turn.
Hilton Hotel 007 Bar, Park Lane, W.1, caters to the younger set. Snack-type meals and dancing from 9:00 until 1:00.
The Mayfair, Berkeley Street, W.1. Reasonable prices in the Chateaubriand Grill, and dancing in the Beachcomber Room (from 8:30–2:00) where alligators swim in a pool, and a tropical storm erupts every night. Also unique Chinese-Polynesian Restaurant. Downstairs Room is for snacks (plus singers), 10–2. The Cinema (classic films and cocktails) and Theatre (satirical revues) are open to members and hotel guests only. Prices average about £3 ($6.00), with wine.
Villa Dei Cesari, 135 Grosvenor Road, S.W. 1. A converted warehouse overlooking the Thames. Continental food. Closed Mondays. Open 7:00–3:00.
Quaglino's, 16 Bury Street, S.W.1. The debutantes' haunt of the '30's, Quags still retains great charm with live trees, glistening chandeliers, good food and music. Set dinner £5.50; open till 2:00 a.m. Saturdays.
The Savoy, Strand, W.C.2, is still the glittering, opulent place you imagine it to be, and just right for a party of half a dozen or so, if price is no particular object. Hours 9:15–2:00, dinner-dance minimum £5.50. Midnight cabaret with Savoy Dancers.
The Stork Room, 99 Regent Street, W.1. The accent is supposedly American but the hours are for night owls. £1.50 cover charge; dinner about £5, dancing 9:00 to 4:30; shows at 10:45 and 1:45.
The Talk of the Town, Hippodrome Corner, Charing Cross Square, W.C. 2. A continuous floor show from 9:30 to midnight. The whole thing is organized with great skill. Dinner-dance. Open 7:30 to 1:15.

The Local, an English institution

NIGHT CLUBS

These clubs require membership for admission, but this usually means paying a fee of between £1.50 and £15, completing a form, and becoming a member 48 hours later. Most are open late (till about 3:30 A.M.), and many have hostesses for dancing. Although most offer meals, eating is not obligatory.

The Astor, Lansdowne Place, Berkeley Square, W.1. Has great floor shows and is highly popular. Subscription £1.10 ($2.20). Open 10:00–3:30; cabaret at 1.

The Blue Angel, 14 Berkeley Square, W.1. Debs and dates, "in" music and out-of-this-world terpsichore. Entrance fee for overseas visitors, £1 ($2.00).

The Cabaret Club, 16 Beak Street, W.1 has one of the loveliest chorus lines in London. Subscription is £2.20 ($4.40) and entrance is £3.30 ($6.60). Hours: 8:00 to 3:00; dancing from 8:00, floor show, 10:00 and 1:00.

Churchill's of Bond Street, 160 New Bond Street, W.1. Cover charge £1.65, dinner £7.50 ($15). Dancing from 9:00, cabaret 11:00 and 1:00, closes 4:00. One of the most popular of all London night spots. Stags welcomed by lissome lovelies.

The Copacabana, 177 Regent Street, W.1. Its proprietor is Sammy Hassan, usually on hand supervising. Membership is £1.50. For £4 you can dine and dance (partners available), or just dance for £2. Dancing 10:00 to 3:30. Floor show at 10:45. Fine food.

Eve, 189 Regent Street, W.1, has dancing from nine in the evening until four in the morning, with floor shows at 10:30 and 1:00. Membership, £1.50 ($3.00), entrance fee £2 ($4.00).

Ginza, 16 Great Newport Street, W.C.2. Dancing to a western trio with Japanese singers, an occasional belly dancer and Japanese food. Quiet, informal atmosphere. Membership £2. Token entrance fee.

Murray's Cabaret Club, Beak Street, W.1. Dancing from 9:00 to 3:30 (partners). Famous for beautiful nudes mirrored in a fish bowl in the bar, Murray's also has glamourous floorshows at 10:15 and 1:15. Membership and entrance both £2.

The Playboy Club, 45 Park Lane, W.1. Bunnies in London in familiar format: a disco, five restaurants, blackjack, roulette, craps. Open 11 A.M. until 4 A.M. Membership £11.

Houses of Parliament, Big Ben, and Westminster Bridge

For many years the home of England's famous theatre company, The Old Vic is slated for demolition in the near future.

Gargoyle, 69 Dean Street, W. 1. Dancing and cabaret. Open Monday through Friday, 11:30 P.M. to 3:30 A.M.

A cover charge and overseas visitors admitted as temporary members. There is also a **Gargoyle Strip Club**—to some people a 1970's anomaly.

ROOF DANCING

Roof Restaurant, Hilton Hotel, W. 1. 27th Floor. Extremely comfortable with beautiful view. French cooking, excellent service, dancing to live music. Closed Sunday. Dinner, £7. **Royal Garden Hotel,** Kensington High St., W. 8. View all across Kensington Gardens to Hyde Park. Two bands plus string ensemble. French cooking. Closed Sunday. Dinner, £10.

JAZZ, SKIFFLE, AND ROCK

There is no question about England's contribution to the world of contemporary music—the Beatles even have the honor of being represented by waxwork figures in Mme. Tussaud's museum. There are hundreds of similar groups, and they have unleashed a pretty aggressive age of sound, a mixture of jazz, rock n' roll and even the plaintive strains of Indian music.

But solid, traditional jazz remains, and some of the best can be heard flourishing in the basements of Soho, but a few clubs may be found tucked away in other parts of town. The two biggest clubs are near neighbors.

The Club 100, 100 Oxford Street, used to be Humphrey Lyttelton's Jazz Club. Old Etonian Lyttelton still plays here sometimes. The 100 Club features some of the biggest names in what hip Britons call "trad jazz": Chris Barber, George Melly, Kenny Ball, Alex Walsh,

Entertainment and Nightlife 111

Ackerbilk, Max Collie. Entrance fee varies with band. Yearly membership costs £1.00. The 100 Club is open from 7:30 to 11:00 weekday nights, to midnight on Fridays, and to 1:00 on Saturdays. The club is licensed, and it serves Chinese food.

The Marquee Club, calling itself a music center, has superb new premises at 90 Wardour Street, and is the official club of the National Jazz Federation. There you can hear rhythm and blues, as well as the moddest of mod groups; The Marquee is where groups like the Who and the Stones get their start! The entrance fee is less than £1.00; there is no membership fee. The hours are 7:00 to 11:00 weekdays; it remains open until midnight on Saturday. The club is licensed. For the names of musicians performing at both clubs, check the *Melody Maker Magazine,* out every Thursday and costing 10p.

JAZZ SPOTS

For the connoisseur: *Ronnie Scott's Jazz Club,* 47 Frith Street, W. 1. The best British, American, and Continental groups, with Pete King and Ronnie Scott resident. The place is really a jazz night club, with excellent cuisine at reasonable prices. 8:30 to 3:00 nightly. Closed Sundays. Entrance is £2 for nonmembers (slightly more on weekends), and memberships (which entitles you to reduced admission fees), cost £3.30. Better still, make the tour: from Oxford Circus, walk along Oxford Street to Wardour Street; follow Wardour, turn left at Old Compton Street and take that to Cambridge Circus; cross Shaftesbury Avenue and turn left on Gerrard Street. Somewhere along the way you'll hear the sounds you want to hear more of.

Nicholson's London Guide states that London discotheques are for the "affluent young, new celebrities and the fashionable" which makes them certainly sound worth a visit. Try: *Revolution,* 14 Bruton Place, W. 1; *Tramps,* 40 Jermyn St., W. 1, 9:00 till 4:00; *Scotch of St. James,* 13 Mason's Yard Duke Street, St. James St., W. 1 (with a good restaurant); *Anthea's,* Foubert's Place, Carnaby Street, W.1; entrance fee £1.50, open till 3:00. *007 Night Spot,* London Hilton, Park Lane W.1; Disco changes with small groups. No entrance fee, open 8:00–3:00. *Saddle Room Club,* 7 Hamilton Place, W.1; London's first disco. Membership £10 per year. Entrance fee hovers around £1.00. Open till 4:00. *Samantha's,* 3 New Burlington Street, W.1, has strobe lights, psychedelic sound and color. For the young. Entrance costs £1.50, open late. *Sundown,* 157 Charing Cross Road, W.C.2 is biggest in London with a resident disk jockey plus a live group. Guest performers most nights, reasonable entrance fee, closing times vary according to night in week. Closed Sunday and Monday.

Last, a few of London's *Bistrotheques* (dine and dance in updated style!) *Fanny's Bistro,* 51 Maddox St., W. 1, 7:30 till 3:00; *Stable,* 123 Cromwell Rd., S.W. 7, French food and disco dancing, 6:30–2:30.

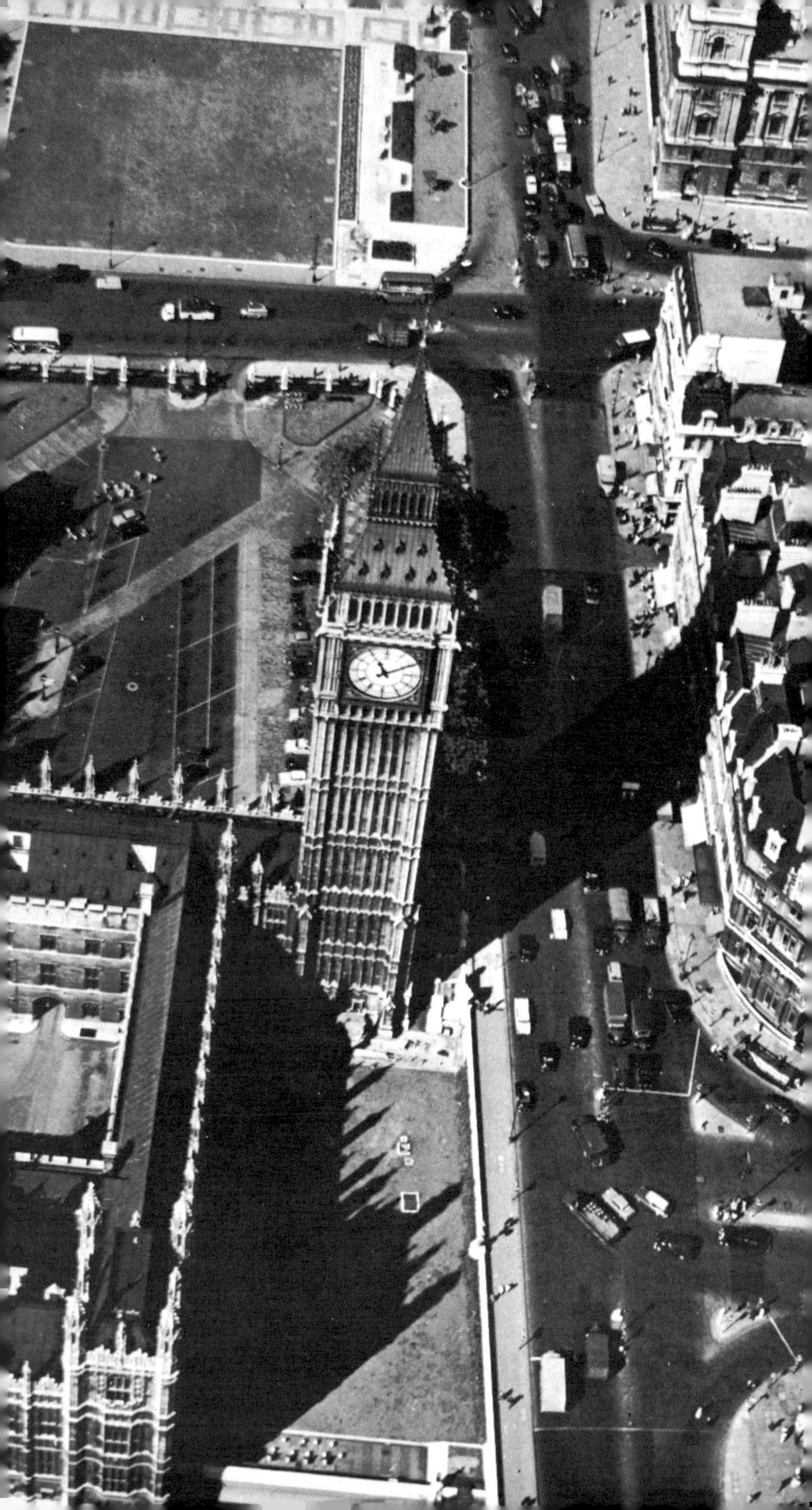

CHAPTER *10*

SHOPPING: FROM PINS TO ELEPHANTS

In London, shopping is not distinct from sight-seeing; it is an agreeable extension of that activity. The city is, after all, the showcase of a "nation of shopkeepers." As the Cockneys boast, you can buy, in London, "everything from pins to elly-phants." It is assumed, however, that most visitors will not be in the market for the second of these items (prices are lower in West Africa), and will only incidentally be spending their pin money on the first.

What are the quality goods in which Britain excels? There are, for a starter, the many items which make up a complete male wardrobe—from ties to raincoats and from hats to shoes. There are accessories and sports equipment, particularly those in which leather is utilized. There are superbly soft, beautiful and long-lasting natural materials—woolens and others—from which clothing for both sexes and all ages can be fashioned by the world's most expert tailors. There are sweaters and skirts, scarves, gloves, stockings and shoes for women to wear, and fine antique jewelry for them to deck themselves out in. For the household, there are exquisitely wrought objects of china (Wedgwood and Lowestoft, for example), porcelain, silver and gold; furniture, both antique (e.g., Chippendale) and modern; rugs, tapestries, linens, and wool blankets. There are chocolates and biscuits, marmalade and preserves, Rolls Royces and sports cars, whiskeys (Scotch) and gins (London). There are bicycles, books, firearms, fishing tackle, pewterware, pipes, plum puddings...

Is shopping an expensive proposition in London? Not for most things, by American standards, though there are exceptions. Purchase tax, levied at varying rates, boosts the price of many articles,

London, mid morning: traffic rushes by Big Ben

114 London

particularly in the luxury class. This need not concern you unduly, however, as visitors can avoid paying purchase tax with perfect legality. You must simply take goods out of the country within three months of the purchase date, and be able to produce both goods and sales slips for the customs inspectors if requested.

But won't the shops send my purchases direct to my home in the U.S.? They will indeed. British Customs, moreover, will normally permit you to take or send out any amount of loot within reason, and the American Customs will let you bring in foreign goods worth up to $100 (£50.00). Hold on to your receipts in case of argument. Getting certain very special articles, e.g., Old Masters, out of Britain is not quite so simple; you might have to procure a license to bring them out from the Department of Trade and Industry, Export Licensing Branch, Norman Shaw North Building, Derby Gate, Victoria Embankment, S.W. 1. Dial 930-4349 if in any doubt.

For information on British Customs regulations contact the Secretary, Customs and Excise, King's Beam House, Mark Lane, E.C.3 (626–1515). On all other shopping questions, feel free to consult the B.T.A., 64–65 St. James's Street, S.W. 1 (629-9191). And before you set out, cash or travelers' checks in hand, do look in at the Craft Centre and Design Centre for important last-minute inspirations. The shield indicates that the shop honors the American Express Credit Card.

MAIN SHOPPING AREAS

London, as has been said, is a conglomerate of large and small communities. Each of these has its own shopping center, supplying the everyday requirements of residents and visitors. But central London—specifically, the West End—contains certain communities which are, to all intents and purposes, made up entirely of shops. To these come people from the far corners of the earth in search of the best that Britain has to offer.

The Bond Street area, in the heart of eastern Mayfair, is unquestionably the most exclusive (and expensive) shopping ground in the whole of the British Commonwealth. This is London's Fifth Avenue and 57th Street, trafficking in much the same kind of merchandise. As noted earlier, art galleries abound here, but so do jewelers, goldsmiths and silversmiths, and world-famous shops dealing in glass, china, porcelain, leather goods, tweeds, linens, knitwear, wool and cashmere.

Bond Street is called "New" throughout most of its course southward from Oxford Street, becoming "Old" before it expires at Piccadilly. East of Bond Street, and roughly parallel, lies the majestic curve of Regent Street, running north from one Circus (Piccadilly) to another (Oxford). Here the shops tend to be larger, and the articles displayed in the windows tend to have price tags attached. Regent Street is renowned for many categories of quality goods, but chiefly, perhaps, for clothes. Appropriately enough, Savile Row, synonymous everywhere for fine British tailoring, lies just off it in the direction of Bond Street. On the other side of Regent Street, in Soho, is Carnaby Street, the opposite extreme from the conservatism of Savile Row. The atmosphere is carnival-like; the clothes are wildly cut, brilliantly colored and cheap, for they were brought into fashion by the rebellious, energetic working-class young, who strongly proclaim, in dress, in long hair and, no doubt, in ideas, that they belong to an altogether new generation. Mod fashion changes even faster than Paris fashion, though, and Carnaby Street shows signs of beginning to suffer from over-exposure. Still, it's just behind Liberty's, and a five minute stroll along it will at least give you the right to dismiss it as over-rated.

Broad Piccadilly runs east and west, touching on both Regent and Bond Streets. South of it is St. James's. Like Regent Street, this area (taking in Lower Regent Street and Haymarket) includes large, high-grade stores whose names are honored everywhere; it boasts a distinctive feature, too, in its magnificent arcades, lined with shops selling all manner of stylish merchandise. In this area more than any other, the smaller establishments are likely to be old, reliable specialists' firms dealing in masculine accouterments; the atmosphere of tradition in some of them is almost palpable.

Parallel to Piccadilly, linking the top ends of Regent and Bond Streets, is London's busiest thoroughfare, Oxford Street. Along it, from Tottenham Court Road to Marble Arch, are some of the biggest stores and department stores in the world. Oxford Street is *the* shopping area of London, far more important to the average Londoner and his country cousins than any other.

Knightsbridge, south of Hyde Park, lies southwest of all the foregoing areas. If Piccadilly-St. James's is mainly for men, this area, hard by fashionable Belgravia and taking in Beauchamp Place and Sloane Street, favors the distaff side. The main street of neighboring Chelsea, to the south, the King's Road, has shops of all kinds, but is particularly good for *with-it clothing and antiques.*

Kensington has become more and more popular with visitors to London, first for its many and various antique merchants (furniture, jewelry, porcelain, silver, clocks, etc.) and second, for its innumerable—and sprouting all the time—clothing boutiques. Both specialties are concentrated along Kensington Church Street and Kensington High Street.

116 London

FOR SHOPPERS IN A HURRY

Ideally, London shopping should be in the nature of a leisurely excursion. But if you simply haven't got the time, don't worry; you can still be sure of getting exactly the right thing for Cousin Bill or Aunt Janet even if you have only half an hour to spare.

Go to **Harrods**. This astonishing emporium in Knightsbridge comes as close to being all things to all men, women and children as any store on earth. Its atmosphere is opulent, serene and thoroughly agreeable, and the languid-looking young salesclerk who is so genuinely pleased to see you will spring into action at your command and hand you your parcel before you know what's happened. Prices are not low (though not wildly out of line, either); but you can be just about certain, whatever you buy there, that you wouldn't have found better quality if you had trudged all over central London in search of it.

OTHER MAJOR STORES

In addition to Harrods, London has at least as many more large stores as the Union has states. A few are "universal," the rest cater to one or the other of the sexes.

BOND STREET AREA
Fenwicks, 63 New Bond St., W.1. For trendy, inexpensive women's clothes and excellent accessories. Bright, somewhat cramped, with a cheery restaurant.

REGENT STREET AREA
Dickins and Jones, 224-244 Regent St., W.1. One of the best in London for fabrics and costume jewelry. Beautifully appointed fashion rooms and pleasant restaurant.

Jaeger, 204 Regent Street, S.W. 1. (plus several branches) Excellent classically styled knits and woolens for men and women.

Liberty, Regent St., W.1. Mixed stone-front and half-timbers on the outside, paneled with dark oak inside; the favorite London store of many discriminating Americans. Its silks, clothes and prints are justly famous, like its Liberty scarves.

PICCADILLY AREA
Fortnum & Mason, 181 Piccadilly, W.1. Visitors on limited budgets will be wise to steer clear of this store, the world's most elegant grocers, as the mouth-watering array of foods (pears in brandy about £4.50, marrons in whisky about £4.25) might easily tempt them to part with a small fortune. In the sumptuous salons upstairs where fashions and fabrics are displayed, the same thing could also happen. Fortnum's restaurant is excellent, and its ground floor "Fountain" a famous meeting place for shoppers.

Tower Yeomen

The Burlington Arcade—fine shops and a friendly Beadle

Simpson's, toward Piccadilly Circus. Stocks distinctive clothes for men and women; it carries a complete selection of sports outfits and equipment as well. Good restaurant and bar.

Piccadilly's two arcades, particularly the historic **Burlington Arcade** (world's longest and oldest—opened 1819) should on no account be missed by shoppers, window-shoppers, or just plain sight-seers.

Oxford Street Area

Bourne and Hollingsworth, Oxford St., W.1. Advertises itself as "one of London's great department stores," and that is just what it is. Excellent for haberdashery and household furnishings.

Debenham and Freebody, 27 Wigmore St., W.1. A leading quality store for "ladies"; its heavy, rather somber paneling accents its reliability. Linen Drapers to the Queen and the Queen Mother.

D. H. Evans, 318 Oxford Street (near Bond Street). Calls itself London's most modern shop. It has a broad range of medium-priced clothing arrayed for easy viewing.

John Lewis, just east along Oxford Street. Has a large (and brand-new) store-front and one of the very largest (and best) fabric departments in town.

Marks and Spencer, 169 and 458 Oxford St., W.1. A huge store. It is also hugely popular, presumably because it is one of the least expensive places in the country to buy most things, especially feminine clothing.

Marshall and Snelgrove, Oxford Street. One of London's venerable stores, it was recently rebuilt in modern style. Good gowns and coats and a famous artificial flowers section.

Peter Robinson, in the Strand. Specializes in better clothes for women and inexpensive models of the very latest fashions for young girls.

Selfridges, Oxford Street toward Marble Arch. The biggest of all, with over 200 departments catering to every (respectable) human whim: a department store in the fullest sense which also offers many services not usually found in such stores (keys made, shoes re-soled, pens repaired).

Knightsbridge Area

Peter Jones, on Sloane Square, S.W.1. Boasts the best-looking building of any London store. Inside (ground floor) is a vast array of good modern china, crockery and porcelain. Immense variety, courteous staff, and considerable imagination in its displays. Often compared to Bloomingdale's in New York. Its motto—"Never Knowingly Undersold"—means that if you find an item cheaper elsewhere, Peter Jones will refund the difference.

Harvey Nichols, 109 Knightsbridge, S.W.1. Carries an immense assortment of clothes for women and children, as well as furnishings.

118 London

KENSINGTON HIGH STREET

Barkers, on both sides of the street is the biggest; its departments vary greatly, but the new Food Hall is an unqualified success. Same ownership as Harrod's; many of the same lines.
Marks & Spencers, Kensington High Street, W.8. Another branch of this unique department store where duchesses vie with working girls for some of the best buys in town. Look for men's cashmeres at one third the usual price, or stylish washable tartan skirts for girls. Merchandise cannot be tried on, but exchanges are easy.

Scotch House, London

FOR SPECIALIST SHOPPERS

In London you can buy Japanese crafts (Mitsukiku, 15 Old Brompton Road, S.W. 7), antique dolls (Dimples and Sawdust, 156 Kensington Church Street, W. 8), or meteorites (Gregory Bottley, 30 Old Church Street, S.W. 3). The places that specialize in somewhat less *special* merchandise are so numerous that it would be impossible to list even all the best under each category, let alone all of them. So there we are. Categories of merchandise in the selection that follows have been pruned to those in which most visiting Americans might be interested. Considerations like accessibility have played a part in choosing the shops. You might want to compare this list with that of a seasoned Londonophile, but you won't go wrong at any of the spots below.

Antiques. Good places for browsing in search of just about anything in this line are the King's Road and Fulham Road, S.W.3, in Chelsea; Beauchamp Place, S.W.1, in Knightsbridge; Church Street, W.8, in Kensington; and St. Christopher Place, W.1, off Wigmore Street in Marylebone. Prints, samplers, ormolu clocks, brassware and Victorian bric-a-brac. Wares often displayed on the sidewalk; prices usually marked.

Books. For new books, try the nearest branch of *W. H. Smith and Sons.* This firm has bookstalls in all railway stations and almost all tube stations. Or try one of the best bookshops in town, *Hatchard's,* 187 Piccadilly, W.1.

As noted earlier, Charing Cross Road, W.C.2, is, with Cecil Court just off it, the heartland of the trade in new and secondhand books. Largest of the ten bookshops in this area (or anywhere else, for that matter) is world-famous *Foyle's,* at 119 Charing Cross Road. *Zwemmers,* at No. 76, specializes in art books. Paperbacks are the specialty of *Ascroft and Daw* (No. 83). *Maggs Brothers* (50 Berkeley Square, W.1) are the best-known antiquarian booksellers in Europe, and other rare items can be found at *Alec Tiranti,* 72 Charlotte Street, W.1, in Soho, and at *Sotheran,* 2 Sackville Street, W.1, just off Piccadilly.

Cars. Inspecting the latest models of British cars is a simple matter, since the main showrooms are conveniently grouped together. Start at Piccadilly, W.1. At Devonshire House you will find the Rover and **the cars of the Chrysler Group: Humbers, Hillmans, Sunbeams and**

Shopping: From Pins to Elephants

Simcas. Austins, Daimlers, Wolseleys, Morrises, MGs and Triumphs are on view at British Leyland Motors Corp. headquarters, No. 41. Jaguars lurk at No. 88. Just a few blocks north in Berkeley Square, W.1, where no nightingales sing are the showrooms of Jack Barclay, Ltd., which buzz with awed comments on the impressively soundless Bentleys and Rolls-Royces.

China, Glass and Porcelain. For china, you could hardly do better than *Gered Wedgewood,* 158 Regent Street, W.1, who keep more than 200 patterns in stock and carry several other lines as well. For china *and* glass, try *The General Trading Co.,* China Department, 144 Sloane Street, S.W.1. *Lawleys,* 154 Regent Street, W.1; and *Thomas Goode,* 19 South Audley Street, W.1. Best for porcelain (but very expensive) are the *Antique Porcelain Company,* 149 New Bond Street, W.1., and *J. and E. D. Vandekar,* 138 Brompton Road, S.W.3. Best *stores* for all three (but contemporary) are *Peter Jones* and *John Lewis.*

Fabrics. Britain's fabulous woolens, including soft cashmeres and sturdy tweeds, have for centuries been recognized around the world as the finest of their kind. These materials can be obtained from department stores, from the tailor who runs up a suit or a coat for you, or from shops specializing in their sale. *Charles S. White,* 245 Regent Street, W.1., carries lots of everything but specializes in worsteds. For tweeds, try *The Scotch House,* 2 Brompton Road, S.W.1 (hand-woven by the islanders of Harris and Skye). More addresses: *W. Bill,* 93 New Bond Street, W.1 (tweeds, suitings, cashmere sweaters); *Hunt & Winterbotham,* 4 Old Bond Street, W.1; *Allan of Duke Street,* 56 Duke Street, W.1; *Racsons,* 108 Jermyn Street, W.1. Many London Shops also handle silks (mostly imported, though Britain's silk industry is growing). See *Gasmey,* 33 Brook Street, W.1.

Fashion Houses. The Big Three

Marks and Spencer and Selfridges dominate one end of Oxford Street, London's main shopping thoroughfare.

among Britain's fashion designers are *Hardy Amies*, 14 Savile Row, W.1; *Norman Hartnell*, 26 Bruton Street, W. 1; *Belleville Sassoon*, 73 Pavilion Road, S.W. 1; and other top-bracketers include *Browns*, 25 South Moulton Street, W. 1; *Jap*, 20 Brompton Road, S.W. 1; *Thea Porter Decorations*, 8 Greek Street, W. 1; *Yves St. Laurent's "Rive Gauche,"* 113 New Bond Street, W. 1, and *John Cavanagh*, 26 Curzon St., W. 1. Most men's tailors, such as *Blades*, 8 Burlington Gardens, Savile Row, W. 1, will make up women's suits—for a price!

Foodstuffs. If *Fortnum and Mason* and *Harrods* haven't heard of it, it probably doesn't exist. Among the good gustatory buys in Britain (of the kind you can take home with you, providing you don't devour them en route) are biscuits, cheese and preserves. Best for cheese is *Paxton and Whitfield*, 93 Jermyn Street, S.W.1. And don't forget chocolates, hand-made and *extremely* good. Treat yourself at *Charbonnel and Walker*, 31 Old Bond Street, W.1, or *Prestat*, 24 South Moulton Street, W.1.

Gold and Silver. The Bond Street area, the King's Road and other places are rich with shops dealing in precious metals. Nevertheless the interested visitor is advised as a first step to head for 65/66 Chancery Lane, W.C.2, in the City, where, in vaults two floors underground, about thirty dealers have set up shop. On Saturdays, try the Portobello Road (see "Street Markets" below).

Kilts, etc. You can be fitted out with the Scottish national costume in all its splendor by the fascinating *Scotch House*, 2-10 Brompton Road, S.W. 1, at the beginning of the Brompton Road. Prices are not exorbitant, and of course, there are tartans by the yard.

"Worth twice as much an' I'll sell it for half!"—Petticoat Lane

Dickens' House at No. 48 Doughty Street.

Knitwear. This feature of British life is not only something to write home about but to *wear* home, too. *Berk,* at 46/49 Burlington Arcade, W.1., has shetlands and Irish Arran hand knits as well as a complete line of cashmeres. *Town and Country Clothes* at 14 New Bond Street, W.1., will mix and match knits for every part of the body. *Noble Jones,* 12-14 Burlington Arcade, W.1. is another good address for woolies, as is *N. Peal,* in the Burlington Arcade, W.1, which stocks knitwear and cashmere sweaters for the small fry as well as adults. Practically all the department stores have big sections devoted exclusively to this line.

Leather Goods. Department stores, again, stock a wide variety of articles in leather, a craft which in this country amounts almost to a *mystique*. For an unusual gift, seek out the leather pigs at *Liberty*, exclusive with them. Or try *Asprey,* 164–169 New Bond Street, W.1, for something smaller. *The Sheepskin Shop,* 435 Oxford Street, and *Skin,* 120a King's Road, specialize in clothing. *W. & H. Gidden,* 74 New Oxford Street, W.C.1, and 15d Clifford Street, W.1, have been the experts at supplying all horsy things since they were tanners and curriers to George III. Beautiful leather trousers and skirts are sold at *Cordoba,* 134 New Bond Street, W.1, and for luxury bags and shoes try *Finnigans,* 198 Sloane Street, S.W.1; *Gucci,* 172 New Bond Street, W.1; or *Loewe,* 25 Old Bond Street, W.1.

Linen and Lace. As far as the U.K. is concerned, this craft stems principally from John Bull's other island. *The White House,* 51 New Bond Street, W.1, is the top shop for linens, but there are a number of smaller places specializing in all aspects of this line. Visit the *Irish Linen Co.,* 35-36 Burlington Arcade, W.1; *Givan's Irish Linen Stores,* 207 King's Road, S.W.3; the *National Linen Co.,* 130 New Bond Street, W.1; or *The Ireland House,* 150 New Bond Street, for handmade products of all kinds.

Men's Hats. 6 St. James's Street, S.W.1, James Lock are *the* hatters. This 18th-century shop, with its fascinating window display of old models, is worth a visit on that account alone. If you venture inside, keep in mind that what we call a derby and the British a bowler is known here as a Coke. It comes in three types. Suit yourself, but if the impulse to go native gets too strong to resist, remember that your uniform won't be complete without the mandatory, tightly rolled umbrella (see "Umbrellas").

The men's departments of the big stores can fit you out, of course (*Harrods* or *Simpson's,* for example). *Austin Reed,* 103 Regent Street, W.1, carries a wide selection of headgear.

Or try *Burberrys,* 18 Haymarket, S.W.1, for the marvelous tweed "deerstalker" cap beloved of Sherlock Holmes.

Men's Tailors and Outfitters. Who are the best tailors in London? Only a committee of dedicated local dandies could answer that one with authority, and even then their replies would reflect personal crotchets. You can, however, be comfortably certain of satisfaction just about anywhere in the West End. On the other hand, unless you can get the advice of someone whose taste you thoroughly trust, it will probably be best to stick to the larger places, which are, after all, quite accustomed to providing for visiting clients who haven't time to spare for extra fittings. Any of the establishments listed below can fit you out to your specifications:

Airey & Wheeler, 129 Regent Street, W.1, and 44 Piccadilly, W.1; *Benson, Perry & Whitley,* 9 Cork Street, W. 1; S. Fisher, 22–23 and 42 Burlington Arcade, W. 1 (especially for fancy waistcoats); *Hawkes* ("Hawkes of Savile Row"), 1 Savile Row, W. 1; *Pope & Bradley,* 35 Dover Street, W. 1, *Austin Reed, Burberrys, Harrods,* and *Simpson's* can "do" you in minimum time.

Pewter. *Harrods, Libertys,* and *Selfridges* stock large amounts of pewterware. So do most jewelers. The leading specialty shop in London, however, is the *Pewter Shop,* Burlington Arcade, W.1. (Also see "Antiques.")

Raincoats. For the supreme craftsmen in this field—whose excellence no doubt owes much to the British climate—we need not go beyond the first two letters of the alphabet. *Aquascutum* is at 100 Regent Street, W.1; *Burberrys* at 18 Haymarket, S.W.1. Enough said.

Shirts. You can have shirts made to your measure and specifications from the material of your choosing by any of the following West End establishments: *Beale & Inman,* 131 New Bond Street, W.1; *Dare & Dolphin,* 90 Piccadilly, W. 1; *Hawes & Curtis,* 2 Burlington Gardens, W. 1; *Harvie and Hudson,* 77 and 97 Jermyn Street, S.W. 1; or *Turnbull & Asser,* 71 Jermyn Street, W. 1. Or if you prefer, consult the large men's stores and/or the men's departments of the department stores.

Shoes. Shoes are a good buy at *all* quality shops in Britain. Men who insist on having a pair made to measure can betake themselves to *Alan McAfee,* 38 Dover Street, W.1.

No. 10 Downing Street, residence of the Prime Minister

Shopping: From Pins to Elephants

and 73 Knightsbridge, S.W. 1. Or: *Henry Maxwell,* 177 New Bond Street, W. 1; *John Lobb,* 9 St. James's Street, S.W. 1; *Church & Co.,* 58 Burlington Arcade, W. 1. Excellent ready-to-wear footgear can be found at leading department stores and men's stores.

Hard-to-please women are advised to try any of the following: *Kurt Geiger,* 95 New Bond St., W. 1, 6 Sloane Street, S.W. 1. *Elliott's,* 76 New Bond St., W. 1, 132 King's Road, S.W. 3; *Bally,* 260 Regent St., W. 1 (and branches); *Rayne,* 57 Brompton Rd., S.W. 3, 15 Old Bond St., W. 1; *Gamba,* 55 Beauchamp Place, S.W. 3.

London specializes in made-to-order boots. An excellent source is *The Chelsea Cobbler,* 33 Sackville St., W. 1, and 165 Draycott Avenue, S.W. 3. Less costly varieties can be found along the King's Road, and Kensington High Street, both ready-to-wear and made to order.

Ties. Anywhere and everywhere. But *do* avoid those stripes that stand for other people's old schools and regiments.

Tobacco and Smokers' Accessories. The best-known shop for smokers is *Alfred Dunhill,* 30 Duke Street, S.W.1, but the most interesting is *Fribourg & Treyer* at 4 Haymarket, S.W.1, (founded 1720). Also: *Inderwick,* 45 Carnaby Street, W.1; the *Astleys,* 109 Jermyn Street, S.W. 1, who pride themselves on their unique collections of new and old pipes.

Umbrellas and Walking Sticks. All department stores that traffic in gentlemen's requisites and all good men's stores can help you here, but go first to *the* place for this kind of thing: *Swaine, Adeney, Brigg & Sons,* 185 Piccadilly, W.1.

Street Markets. Shoppers on the lookout for bargains should on no account miss an opportunity to visit London's street markets. In a low-to-no-overhead lashup like this, in which goods change hands with lightning speed (too fast, sometimes, for a barrow-owner to appraise his latest acquisitions at their proper value), there's no telling what you may wind up with, particularly if you're prepared to haggle. But cupidity is only one of the lures. More important for adventurous spirits is the excitement of the spectacle itself.

These open-air bazaars bring the London of Dickens to life—and up-to-date. You will find yourself fascinated by the clutter and clatter, the spiels of the pitchmen, the transient expressions of the ordinary citizens as they gawk and ogle, question, reject and finally shuffle along to the next barrow to start again.

On weekdays, the big markets (for everything) are in Lower Marsh and the Cut, S.E.1 (off Waterloo Road); Mile End Waste, Whitechapel, E.1; Leather Lane, Holborn, E.C.1; Berwick Street, Soho, W.1; and Lambeth Walk, Lambeth, S.E.1.

Saturday mornings, the earlier the better, is the time to visit the Portobello Road in North Kensington, W.10 and W.11. Bargains are to be found, amidst the hurly-burly, in the way of silver, jewelry, pictures, lace, china, pewter, curios.

But the daddy of all London street markets—quite as colorful, to us foreigners at any rate, as anything in Naples—takes place in Petticoat Lane, Middlesex Street, E.C.1, and neighboring territory of a Sunday morning (best time to visit: between 10:00 and 1:00). Go there yourself (tube stations Aldgate or Aldgate East) and see.

INDEX

Adam, Robert, 74
Adams, John Quincy, 72
Addresses, finding, 55
Admiralty, 65
Admiralty Arch, 64
Agriculture Ministry, 65
Airplane tours, 55
Albert, Prince, 22, 75
Albert Hall, 22
Albert Memorial, 75
André, John, 71
Antiques, 118
Apartments, 87
Art galleries, 33–35
Arts Council Gallery, 34
Auctions, 35

Ballet, 106
Bank of England, 43, 60
Bankside, 26
Bar billiards, 37
Barber, Chris, 111
Battersea Park, 37
Bayswater, 30, 84
Beaverbrook, William, Lord, 42
Bede, The Venerable, 12
Beer, 36, 98
Belgravia, 28, 92
Big Ben, 66
Billingsgate, 39
Bird, Francis, 62
Blackheath Common, 47
Blake, William, 34
Bligh, William, Capt., 72
Bloody Tower, 58
Bloomsbury, 31, 85
Blow, John, 71
Boadicea, Queen, 12
Board of Trade, 114
Boat races, 44, 47
Boat tours, 54–55
Bond Street, 114, 116
Books, 38, 118
Borough Market, 39
Brandon, Henry, 43
British Museum, 40
British Travel and Holidays Ass'n, 33, 77–78, 114
Brompton, 30

Brooks, Phillips, 68
Brown, Sandy, 111
Browning, Robert, 71
Burbage, James, 17
Burke, Edmund, 67
Burns, Robert, 71
Buses, 51, 53, 54
Bushy Park, 46
Buskers, 107

Cade, Jack, 16
Caesar, Julius, 11
Camden Hill, 30
Canute, King, 13
Carnaby Street, 115
Cars, 53–54, 118–19
Carlyle, Thomas, 75
Catharine of Aragon, 68
Caxton, William, 68
Cenotaph, 66
Ceremony of the Keys, 44
Changing of the Guard, 43
Charing Cross, 18
Charles I, 17, 65, 67, 74
Charles II, 18–19, 61, 71, 74
Chaucer, Geoffrey, 71
Chelsea, 29, 92, 102
Chelsea Hospital, 74
Chemin de fer, 38
Chinaware, 119
Chophouses, 94
Christie's, 35
Churches,
   All Hallows, 71–72
   All Saints', 75
   Chelsea Old, 75
   St. Bartholomew-the-Great, 72
   St. Clement Danes, 63
   St. Dunstan's, 63
   St. Ethelburga's, 72
   St. George's, 74
   St. Helen's, 72
   St. James's, 74
   St. Margaret's, 66, 68
   St. Martin's-in-the-Fields, 64
   St. Mary-le-Strand, 63
   St. Mary's, 72

   St. Paul's Cathedral, 25, 60–62
   St. Paul's Church, 64
   St. Peter ad Vincula, 59
   Southwark Cathedral, 26–27, 72
   Temple Church, 63
   Westminster Abbey, 13, 66, 68–71
   Westminster Cathedral, 72
Cibber, Caius Gabriel, 62
City, The, 8, 26
   chophouses, 94
   hotels, 85
   pubs, 101
   wine houses, 103
Cleopatra's Needle, 73
Clock Tower, 66
Clothing, buying, 120 ff.
Coleridge, Samuel Taylor, 71
College of Arms, 72
Commonwealth Inst., 40
Concerts, 106
Conducted tours, 54–55
Cooke, Alistair, 42
Coronation Chair, 18, 70
Courtauld Inst. of Art, 34
Courts of law, 38, 63
Covent Garden, 39, 64
Crafts Centre, 36
Cricket, 47
Cromwell, Oliver, 18, 67
Crosby, John, 75
Crosby Hall, 75
Customs and Excise, 114
Customs regulations, 114

Dance, George, the elder, 60
Dancing, 108–10
Danes, 12–13
Darts, 37
Darwin, Charles, 71
Defence Ministry, 65
Design Centre, 36
Dickens, Charles, 31, 75
Dining (*see* Restaurants)
Disraeli, Benjamin, 71, 74

124

Donne, John, 61, 62
Downing, Sir George, 66
Downing Street, 66
Drinking, 98–99
Drugs, 49
Dryden, John, 71

Earl's Court, 30
Eating (*see* Restaurants)
Edward V, 59
Edward VII, 22
Edward the Confessor, 13, 70
Eleanor's Cross, 18
Elephant and Castle, 27
Elizabeth I, 17
Elizabeth II, 23, 62, 74
Entertainment, 105–11
(*See also* Games; etc.)
Epping Forest, 47
Epstein, Jacob, 46
Eros (statue), 23

Fabrics, 119
Faraday, Michael, 71
Fashion houses, 120
Fawkes, Guy, 45, 67
Ferdinand V, 68
Fleet Street, 63
Foodstuffs, 120
Football, 47
Fox, Charles, 67, 71
Free speech, 36
Furnished apartments, 87

Galeries, 33–34
Games, 37–38, 47–48
Geffrye Museum, 40
Geological Museum, 40
George II, 69
George III, 19
George V, 22
George VI, 23
George Inn, 72
Gibbons, Grinling, 62, 74
Gibbs, James, 64
Gill, Eric, 72
Gin Lane, 20
Gladstone, William, 71
Glassware, 119
Globe Theatre, 17, 26
Gloves, 120
Golf, 47
Gold, 120
Gray's Inn, 75

Great Fire of 1666, 18, 59
Great Plague of 1665–66, 18
Green Park, 46
Green Mansions, 46
Greenwich Park, 47
Gresham, Sir Thomas, 60
Grey, Lady Jane, 59
Greyhound racing, 48
"Griffin, The," 63
Guildhall, 60
Gunpowder Plot, 45
Gwyn, Nell, 19, 74

Hainault Forest, 47
Hallam, Lewis, 64
Hampstead Heath, 46
Hardy, Thomas, 71
Harley Street, 31
Harold, King, 13
Harrods, 116
Harvard, John, 26–27
Hastings, Warren, 67
Hats, men's, 121–22
Hawksmoor, Nicholas, 69
Heine, Heinrich, 9
Henrietta Maria, Queen, 74
Henry I, 14
Henry II, 15
Henry III, 15
Henry VII, 68, 69, 70–71
Henry VIII, 16, 68, 70, 73
History of the World (Raleigh), 59
Discovery, H.M.S., 73
Hogarth, William, 20
Hogarth Agency, 87
Holbein, Hans, 33, 73
Holborn, 31, 85
Holland House, 75
Holmes, Oliver Wendell, 8
Home Office, 65
Horse Guards, 43, 65
Horse racing, 48–49
Hotels, 77–86, 107, 108
Hudson, Henry, 72
Hudson, W. H., 46
Hyde Park, 36, 46, 57

Imperial War Museum, 40
Inns of Court, 31, 63, 75

Isabella I, 68

James I, 17
James II, 19, 64
James, John, 74
Jazz, 110–11
Jewel Tower, 72
Jewish Museum, 40
John, King, 14–15
John the Evangelist, 59
Johnson, Samuel, 31, 72, 75
Jones, Inigo, 17, 74
Jonson, Ben, 71

Kelvin, William, Lord, 71
Kensington, 29–30
hotels, 83–84, 86
pubs, 102
restaurants, 93
shopping in, 115, 118
Kensington Gardens, 46
Kent, William, 65
Kilts, 120
Kipling, Rudyard, 71
Knightsbridge, 28, 115, 117
Knitwear, 121

Lace, 121
Lambeth, 27
Lancaster Gate, 30, 84
Law Courts, 38, 63
Le Sueur, Hubert, 65
Leadenhall Market, 39
Leather goods, 121
Lincoln, Abraham, 66
Lincoln's Inn, 75
Linen, 121
Literature, 38
London Accommodation Bureau, 87
London Bridge, 15–16
London Museum, 40, 75
Longchamp, William, 14
Longfellow, Henry W., 71
Lord Mayor's Show, 45
Lord Privy Seal, 65
Low, David, 42
Lowell, James Russell, 68
Ludgate Circus, 62–63
Lyttleton, Humphrey, 111

125

Macauley, Thomas, 59
Macklin, Charles, 64
Magna Carta, 15
Mansion House, 60
Marble Arch, 30, 36, 75
Markets, 38–39, 123
Marlborough House, 73
Mary I, 17
Marylebone, 31, 93
Matilda, Queen, 14
Mayfair, 28
  hotels, 79
  nightlife, 107 ff.
  restaurants, 90
  shopping, 114, 116
Medical care, 49
Men's clothing, 121–22
Mermaid at Puddle Dock, 106
Milton, John, 71
Money, 50–51
Monolulu, "Prince," 48
Montfort, Simon de, 15
Monument, The, 59–60
More, Sir Thomas, 75
Mounting the Guard, 43
Museums, 40–41

Nash, John, 46
National Gallery, 34, 64
National Portrait Gallery, 34, 64
Natural History Museum, 40
Nelson, Horatio, Viscount, 64
Newspapers, 41–43
Newton, Isaac, 71
Night clubs, 107, 109–10
Nightlife, 105–11
Nixon, Richard, 62
Norden, John, 16
Notting Hill, 30

Old Bailey, 38
Opera, 106
Oxford Street, 115, 117

Paddington, 30
Pageantry, 43–45
Palace of Westminster, 67
Palaces,
  Buckingham, 22, 43, 74
  Banqueting House, 19, 65

Fulham, 75
Kensington, 19, 30, 75
Lambeth, 27, 72
St. James's, 43, 73–74
Whitehall, 65
Palmerston, Henry, 71
Pamela, 20
Parks, 45–47
Parliament, 45, 66–68
Peel, Sir Robert, 21–22, 71
Penn, William, 72
Pepys, Samuel, 19, 45, 66
Peter, St., 68–69
Peter of Colechurch, 15
Pewter, 122
Piccadilly, 23, 116–17
Pimlico, 28–29
Pitt, William, 71
Porcelain, 119
Post Office, 36, 60
Post Office Tower, 25
Pubs, 37, 97–103
Purcell, Henry, 71

Queen's Chapel, 74
Queensway, 30

Racing, 48–49
Rahere (monk), 72
Raincoats, 122
Raleigh, Sir Walter, 59, 68
Regent Street, 116
Regent's Park, 31, 46
Rest rooms, 50
Restaurants, 89–95
  cheap, 95
  chophouses, 94
  dining, dancing, 107–8
  (*See also* Pubs)
Richard I, 14
Richard II, 67
Richard III, 59
Richardson, Samuel, 20
Richmond Park, 46–47
Rignall, Florence, 39
Rima (Epstein), 46
Roman Empire, 11–12
Roosevelt, Theodore, 74
Royal Botanic Gardens, 47
Royal Court Theatre, 106
Royal Exchange, 60

Royal Societies, 34
Ruskin, John, 71

St. Bartholomew's Hospital, 60
Saint-Gaudens, Augustus, 66
St. James's, 28, 73–74
  restaurants, 90
  shopping, 115
St. James's Park, 45
St. John's Wood, 31
St. Marylebone, 31, 93
St. Pancras, 31
Savoy Chapel, 64
Scott, Robert Falcon, 73
Searle, Ronald, 37
Shakespeare, William, 17, 71
Shaw, George Bernard, 22
Shelley, Percy Bysshe, 74
Sheridan, Richard Brinsley, 67
Shirts, 122
Shoes, 122–23
Shopping, 35, 113–23
Shove ha'penny, 37
Sidewalk artists, 49
Silver, 120
Skiffle, 111
Smithfield Market, 39
Smokers' accessories, 123
Snooker, 37
Soane, Sir John, 60, 74
Soccer, 47
Soho, 28, 90–91
Somerset, Edward, Duke of, 64
Somerset House, 63–64
Sotheby's, 35
South Kensington, 30, 93
Southey, Robert, 71
Southwark, 26–27
Speakers' Corner, 30, 36
Spenser, Edmund, 71
Spitalfields Market, 39
Sports, 47–49
Stephen, King, 14
Stock Exchange, 35
Stone of Scone, 70
Street entertainers, 49, 106–7
Street markets, 123
Stuart, Arabella, 71

126

Subway, 51, 52–53
Sweyn, King, 12–13

Tailors, men's, 122
Tate Gallery, 34
Taxis, 51–52
Telephones, 49
Temple, The (*see* Inns of Court)
Temple Bar Memorial, 63
Tennis, 47
Tennyson, Alfred, Lord, 71
Theatre Royal, 106
Theatres, present-day, 105–6
Thomas à Becket, St., 15
Thornhill, Sir James, 62
Ties, 123
Tijou, Jean, 62
Tipping, 51, 78–79
Tobacco, 123
Tomb of the Unknown Warrior, 70
Tours, conducted, 54–55
Tower Bridge, 22
Tower of London, 13, 44, 58–59
Trafalgar Square, 36, 64–65
Traffic, walking in, 51
Transportation, 51–55
Treasury, 65
Trooping the Colour, 44, 65
Tube (subway), 51, 52–53
Turner, Joseph M. W., 34
Tussaud's Waxworks, 41
Tyburn, 75
Tyler, Wat, 16

U.S.I.S. Library, 34
Umbrellas, 123
United States Information Service Library, 34
Universal Aunts, 87

Vaudeville, 106
Velázquez, Diego Rodrigues de Silva y, 41
Victoria, Queen, 22
Victoria and Albert Museum, 40
Victoria area, 28–29
Victoria Palace (theatre), 106
Victoria Park, 47
Victoria Tower, 66

Wakefield Tower, 58
Walking sticks, 123
Wallace Collection, 34
Walpole, Robert, 20
War Office, 65
Washington, George, 65
Watermen's Derby, 44
Wellcome Museum, 41
Wellington, Arthur, 1st Duke of, 41
Wellington Museum, 41
Wesley, John, 75
West End, 31, 79, 99, 114
Westminster, 13, 27–29, 79
Westminster Abbey, 13, 66, 68–71
Westminster Bridge, 16
Westminster Hall, 18, 66, 67
Westminster School, 72
Whitbread's Brewery, 36
White Tower, 13–14, 58
Whitechapel Art Gallery, 34
Wilkes, John, 62–63
William I (the Conqueror), 13
William II (Rufus), 14, 67
William III, 19
Windmill (theatre), 106
Wine houses, 103
Wolfe, James, 71
Wordsworth, William, 71
Wren, Sir Christopher, 18, 59–60 ff., 73 ff.